The Bible On The Living God

The Bible

on the

Living God

by B. VAN IERSEL, S.M.M.

Translated by H. J. VAUGHAN

ST. NORBERT ABBEY PRESS
De Pere, Wisconsin
U. S. A.
1965

Biblical quotations are from the Revised Standard Version of the Bible, copyrighted 1946 and 1952 by the Division of Christian Education, National Council of Churches, and used by permission.

Nihil obstat:

John M. T. Barton, S.T.D., L.S.S.
Censor deputatus

Imprimatur:

Patrick Casey, V. G.
Westminster, England
January 18, 1965

The *Nihil obstat* and *Imprimatur* are a declaration that a book or pamphlet is considered free from doctrinal or moral error. It is not implied that those who have granted the *Nihil obstat* and *Imprimatur* agree with the contents, opinions or statements expressed.

Originally published as *De Bijbel over de Levende God,* J. J. Romen and Zonen, Roermond (1962).

Library of Congress catalogue card number: 65 - 18140

Printed in the United States of America
ST. NORBERT ABBEY PRESS
De Pere, Wisconsin

CONTENTS

FOREWORD

Every Christian has his own image of God and — thanks to the more or less successful efforts of his religious teachers — he even acquires a certain concept of God. However, a widening range of these representations of God and the development of intellectual knowledge are not always accompanied by a deepening awareness of God.

In the books of the Bible it is just the reverse: not only do we look there in vain for a real representation of God, but our search for a definition of God does not yield satisfactory results either; what we do find is that the various authors of these books had an intense awareness of God.

Of the many likely reasons for this, one of the most important is undoubtedly the fact that their lives were governed by a profound piety based on their immediate religious experience. We too can share in this experience of many generations of an entire people by studying the books of sacred Scripture. The books of the New Testament tell us what God did and said in the person of Jesus of Nazareth; those of the Old Testament enable us to prepare ourselves for it. Just as Jacob struggled with the angel of God — and this really means God himself — so we see God in the Old Testament struggling with his chosen people in order to bind it to him. Ancient Israel appears to have regarded this as a struggle to attain a pure conception of Yahweh's identity; anyone, therefore, who takes part in this struggle by reading the Old Testament will be deepening his own awareness of God.

But because various circumstances have estranged us from the Bible and especially the Old Testament, the present-day Christian easily loses his way in this reading and often forgets the real issues. This is why in the 1957 numbers of the periodical *Het Heilig Land (The Holy Land)* several articles were devoted to the collation of the viewpoints, characteristics and highlights of Israel's awareness of God. Not, indeed, as a substitute for reading the Old Testament but as an inducement for readers to pick up the Old Testament themselves and thus enter into the world of ancient Israel's religious experience.

If those articles are published once again it is because I am convinced they will give the readers a knowledge of Yahweh — the God of Israel, who sent his Son and whom we too may call "Father" — that ordinary religious instruction cannot give them; and that the sharing in Israel's experiences will transform their own abstract conception of God into a living reality.

THE AWARENESS OF GOD IN THE OLD TESTAMENT

Anyone who has received a Catholic upbringing never lacks a concept of God. His lessons at school, books and sermons, and particularly the Catechism, have given him an idea, an abstract mental image of God; usually a purely intellectual concept. Nor is he likely to be without material representations of God: an old gentleman with a beard, as in the pictures of the Creation — or maybe even wearing a top hat which makes him look like a good-natured clergyman, as in the film *Green Pastures*. Both a concept and a picture of God can be induced, and it seems to me that in a pronouncedly religious upbringing there lies a danger that a child may either be talked into these things or have them visually suggested without its acquiring a real and lively awareness of God. For the awareness of God — "le sens de Dieu" as the French say — cannot be induced, any more than any other kind of awareness. It can only be acquired by experience. It follows that it lies deeper than any image or concept of God. An object or a person is understood chiefly through the intellect, an image is formed by the imagination; but awareness comes from the depths of man's whole self. Awareness of God comes from the depth of our being.

What strikes us about Israel is that we search in vain through her sacred books, the Old Testament, for something we can call a concept of God, an attempted definition of what or who God is. Representations of God are many because he is often spoken of figuratively — as a father, or a king, or a shepherd. But the Old Testament is full to overflowing of a deep and lively awareness of God. And this is why it is so valuable to read the Old Testament: by taking part in the experiences of Israel we share this awareness of God, thus developing the sense with which we are to experience God in our own lives and in the history of our own times and become aware of God as an ever-present reality. This is precisely what enables us to attain a personal relationship with God.

Of course, in many of the books of the Old Testament this awareness of God is communicated only indirectly and with far less clarity than, for instance, in the Psalms. It seems important, therefore, that we should analyze ancient Israel's awareness of God by examining its assumptions, its main features and chief manifestations. Things immediately obvious in some books can then be used as a background for reading others in which they are less explicit, and thus make it easier for us to get a true picture of what we read in them.

Actually the subject of my discussions could well be given a place in a theology of the Old Testament. But there is no need for the reader to be afraid that technical theological terms will make it difficult for him to understand. Such specialist language, however hallowed, can only be adopted when there is agreement on the content of the terms applied, when these terms cover accurately defined and carefully tested concepts on which those who are going to use them are agreed. But this theological "code," which make it impossible for so many well-meaning believers to enter more deeply into the reality of their religion, was just as unknown to the authors of the books of the Old Testament as it is to them; the Israelites never learned this secret language either. It could hardly be otherwise. One thing you cannot describe them as is theologians. Indeed not all of them were even intellectuals, though many no doubt had an excellent education — such as Moses, who was "instructed in all the wisdom of the Egyptians" (Acts 7:22) (but then, to what extent was he an author in the accepted modern sense of the term?). A case at the other extreme was the prophet Amos, a sheep-farmer and tree-grower. Paul, who received a full rabbinical education, seems to be the only one who can really be called a professional theologian. Perhaps this is why his Epistles are to be classed among the most difficult sections of biblical literature. The knowledge that the majority of the biblical authors were not professional theologians will assure the reader that he will not be faced with an impenetrable mass of theological terms. Nor should he fear the dryness that comes from divisions, distinctions and abstractions. The idea of "divide and conquer" which applies to the realms of science as well as to those of politics, is an invention of the western mind. There is no place for distinctions or abstractions where God is not "thought of" but "lived with." In the Old Testament God is always spoken of concretely. It is only in the Sapiential books, where the influence of Greek philosophy is most strongly felt, that he is spoken of in more general terms. But even there he is not spoken of without emotion, because the individual speaker is never left untouched by what he says about God. In the Old Testament no one ever stands aloof from God to hold him up as an object of knowledge. People are too deeply involved personally for that. What is written in the Old Testament about God is never something outside experience; rather it proceeds from the actual and full reality of experience itself. So it is not God as he is in himself who is written about but the Lord who reveals himself in the wonders of nature and in history.

Of course, like any other picture, this one too has a reverse side. Just because what is said about God is so existential — to use a fashionable word which, indeed, in its original sense, best expresses what I mean — every saying has a limited value and can only be understood if we bear in mind the situation in which it arose. There is no search for forms of expression that will retain their validity however much they are twisted or slanted. There is no attempt to express truth and reality as fully and as adequately as possible. That can only be done if one proceeds systematically, despite the knowledge that where God is concerned complete success is impossible. None of the Old-Testament authors had the kind of mental training that implies. In any case, we should not expect this propensity in eastern minds. They make no attempt to summarize all that can be said about God;

they only try to put into words their own attitude of the moment, the way God reveals himself now, or the demand of a definite moment or well-defined period. This is why in many cases their words contain only a limited amount of truth.

Pascal put this briefly and pithily when he wrote, "The God of the Bible is not a God of philosophers but the God of Abraham, Isaac and Jacob, the God who reveals himself in history as a deliverer."

Finally we must take into account that this makes a development in what God reveals about himself in the Old Testament possible and necessary. Again and again some passage or another illuminates only one, or just a few, of the facets of divine reality. So the whole picture only becomes clear very gradually. God allows himself to become known only bit by bit. The divine food is served out mouthful by mouthful and that is just as well, for otherwise who would be able to digest it? This is another thing that the Christian who picks up the Old Testament should be well aware of. There is a development, an increase in depth and growth, of the Chosen People's awareness of God (sometimes perhaps even a temporary impoverishment). Again and again the reader finds pronouncements about God in the Old Testament which, taken by themselves, are at least onesided and incomplete and require others for a correct appreciation. The best way to put it is perhaps to say that in the Old Testament the awareness of God is repeatedly overtaken by the reality, and that for this reason the faithful of those days stood in greater need of correction and amplification in their ideas than we do.

Usually the awareness of God of an early period is overtaken and excelled by that of a later one, though this development takes place less homogeneously and evenly than might be imagined.

Furthermore, this awareness of God, and especially its expression, is often mixed with alien elements that still need purifying. This is not to be wondered at. The Patriarchs had not always known Yahweh; Israel's prehistory took place in pagan times. And her history proper continues to unfold among pagan peoples. Israel always had too many points of contact with her pagan surroundings to be unaffected by them. It was not only the way she thought that showed an obvious affinity with that of the neighboring peoples but, quite naturally, what she thought. This applies to both religious and secular spheres. The views and practices of ancient Israel were only slowly and gradually purified of what was really pagan in them. This is why we find texts and passages in which this purifying process has been only partially carried out, and viewpoints that are not only unacceptable to a Christian but foreign to Israel in her full spiritual development. Naturally this does not make for an easy understanding of the Old Testament, but it does, on the other hand, enable the reader to take part in Israel's struggle for a pure awareness of God. It helps his own awareness of God to gain in depth and purity.

For ancient Israel Yahweh is a living God in the same way that the gods of the other eastern peoples are living gods for them: "The Lord is the true God; he is the living God and the everlasting King. At his

wrath the earth quakes, and the nations cannot en-
dure his indignation." (Jer. 10:10) We too have been
taught that God lives but when we speak of God's
life we really mean something else; we think particularly of the mysterious and invisible interplay of
knowledge and love whereby the Father sends forth
his Son and both Father and Son generate the Holy
Ghost. For the Israelite and for eastern man in general God's life is visible, manifest and observable.
This is expressed, for instance, in Joshua's words to
the children of Israel:

> Hereby you shall know that the living God is among you,
> and that he will without fail drive out from before you the
> Canaanites, the Hittites, the Hivites, the Perizzites, the
> Girgashites, the Amorites, and the Jebusites. Behold, the ark
> of the covenant of the Lord of all the earth is to pass over
> before you into the Jordan. Now therefore take twelve men
> from the tribes of Israel, from each tribe a man. And when
> the soles of the feet of the priests who bear the ark of the
> Lord, the Lord of all the earth, shall rest in the waters of
> the Jordan, the waters of the Jordan shall be stopped from
> flowing, and the water coming down from above shall stand
> in one heap. [Joshua 3:10-13]

When the Israelite speaks of Yahweh's life he is
thinking of the manifestation of God's activity in history and in nature. He is thinking of God's voice
sounding in the thunder; of God's breath which
brushes over the earth when the wind blows; of the
flashes which he flings through space when it is
lightening. When the Old Testament speaks of God's
life it really means — to put it simply — his concern
with and part in the things he has created and allows
to happen.

2

THE GOD WHO MAKES HISTORY

Modern historiography is chiefly concerned with man. In his efforts to outline intellectual currents or describe conflicts in which one half of the world comes to blows with the other, in his endeavors to show the movements of the masses or trace their evolution through several generations, the historian obviously encounters man. Not only because the masses are made up of people and generations are continued through the survival of people, but also because it is always concrete persons who fashion a given period or create a certain philosophy, whether in the field of politics, culture or religion. The historian — in the sense that we have come to attach to the term — is, in the first place, a judge of people; who describes and explains what people do — individually or collectively — and shows the reasons behind those actions.

We cannot say the same about the kind of historiography which we encounter in the books of the Old Testament. There were, undoubtedly, Old Testament political and religious leaders and personalities who left their stamp on the age they lived in. One thinks of Moses, who gave the Israelites their first laws, led them out of Egypt and made the covenant with

Yahweh; of Joshua, who led the people of Israel into Canaan and made them renew their choice between Yahweh and the Canaanite idols, in Shechem; of the Judges, who intervened in troubled times and took charge of the struggle with the Canaanites whenever these took advantage of the Israelites in moments of indecision. One thinks of Saul, the first king; of David, who made Jerusalem his capital and managed to keep the rival tribes in check, giving them strength in unity; of Solomon, who built the Temple and promoted religious unity in Israel; of the prophets Samuel, Elijah, Elisha, Isaiah and Jeremiah, whose influence on religious life was of the greatest importance. All these figures receive plenty of attention in the Old Testament, but when we look for accurate details about them we find so very little that there is hardly enough to produce a reasonably complete biography of any one of them. The contemporary scene, too, is imperfectly, often sketchily, drawn — without shading or finesse. Furthermore, what little we know about the main characters often has the appearance of a family chronicle. This applies, for instance, to David; various digressions about family feuds take the place of the kind of information we seek. Important events are often briefly touched upon; just as often they are not mentioned at all. For example, we know from extra-biblical sources that the reign of King Omri in the Northern Kingdom (884-873 BC) was a brilliant period in Israel's history, yet we find no mention of it in the Books of Kings; all we learn about Omri is that he was not devout enough.

If we find out little about men, we learn all the

more about God. For ancient Israel, Yahweh is the
Lord of history and this is reflected in the books of
the Old Testament where historiography means primarily the recording of God's actions with and
through men. Along with the realization that men
have their own reasons for what they do or fail to
do, there is a deep consciousness that Yahweh car-
ries out his plans mainly through human actions and
that he, too, is active in the free manifestations of the
human will. Israel's conception of history shows us
that Yahweh was regarded as a living God who had
not withdrawn into heaven but was taking part in the
activities of his creatures, including man, even in his
political activities. So deeply was this thought im-
pressed upon the Israelites that it had a considerable
influence on the portrayal of events, and this is especially so in the books of Joshua and Judges and also
— though to a lesser degree — in those of Samuel and
Kings. Time and again the same pattern recurs: the
people (or the king, which comes to the same thing)
sin and Yahweh punishes them by delivering them
into the hands of their enemies; later they repent
and Yahweh brings deliverance. We know for certain
that this pattern does not always fit in with reality,
yet we find the authors rather naively maintaining
it; but then, they were not primarily concerned with
what was happening, but rather with the lessons
that were to be learned from it. Their history does
not follow the line of human actions but that of
Yahweh's purposes in them; it is redemptive history
because it shows the accomplishment of ancient
Israel's — and the whole world's — salvation.

Yahweh's presence in history is expressed in the simplest way, often by attributing to him events for which men themselves have really been responsible; a process which may on occasion put the inexperienced reader on a false track. When the tribe of Dan sent out spies to examine the land and see where they might establish themselves to best advantage, they arrived near the town of Laish, heartened by what a priest had told them in an oracle. They noticed rich natural resources, living which allowed all to lead carefree lives and, furthermore, that the inhabitants did not appear to have entered into any political or military alliances, so that the tribe would be able to attack the town without running any undue risk. On their return to their fellow tribesmen they interpreted the situation as follows: "God has given it into your hands." (Judges 18:10.) This seems to be more than just a manner of speaking; they really did regard their favorable situation as a dispensation of Yahweh. The capture of a town is another thing that is often attributed to him; thus the Lord, speaking to Joshua about Ai: "Do not fear or be dismayed; take all the fighting men with you, and arise, go up to Ai; see, I have given into your hand the king of Ai, and his people, his city, and his land." (Joshua 8-1) The rest of the chapter clearly indicates that Joshua's strategy has, to a certain extent, been responsible for the course of events; but the actual operations of war which cause a town to fall are not always mentioned and so we may, on occasion, too quickly assume a miraculous intervention on Yahweh's part. Indeed, ancient Israel considered human undertakings to have far less telling effects on the outcome of a situation than Yahweh's, and this is why the latter is often exclusively emphasized.

Ancient Israel's historiography is, in the final analysis, religious historiography, and that in two respects. First: Those events which are of religious significance are the ones that are chiefly mentioned and given prominence. If we learn such a lot about the complications in David's family, it is not because they are in themselves important; their real importance lies in their connection with the succession and, therefore, with Yahweh's promise to David that his house would be chosen from all the others and would reign forever. With Solomon the stories are centered on the building of the Temple and, in the same way, the story of his life emphasizes the aspects that bear religious importance. For an historian whose interest also covers more mundane events, this method leaves a lot to be desired; but, as far as the redemptive events are concerned, they are illuminated from every possible angle. Second: Writing history is, in a sense, making a proclamation. In the Old Testament it is Yahweh's mighty deeds that are proclaimed, not because they are all that interesting in themselves — historians delve into the past, not for its own sake so much as for its lessons, so that they may be passed on to the readers — but because in those deeds the people of Israel will know their own God. They will learn that Yahweh's way with their forefathers will also be his way with them. What a profound lesson remembering Yahweh's mighty deeds proves to be for Israel is made clear by some of the Psalms —

44, 78, 105, and 136, for example. The past is not dead; it lives on in every single moment and throws light on the present-day situation; Yahweh's faithfulness and grace remain unchanged.

This is not to say that all we read is edifying; on the contrary. Indeed, the people's faithlessness occupies an important place and there is hardly a sin we do not find mentioned; Yahweh's faithfulness is met by the people's faithlessness. This again receives ample treatment, with no attempt to play it down — the better to glorify Yahweh's grace; since it shows that, despite everything, he goes on taking pity on Israel. And is it not a fact also that these sins are never entirely of the past? On the other hand, the Chosen People are, to some extent, hereditarily tainted by them; though not directly responsible for the sins of their fathers, the effects of them are nevertheless felt for many a year. On the other, the Israelite recognizes himself all too often in the sinfulness of the fathers. Thus, the place of sin in the teaching he receives will lead him to repentance.

To call Yahweh the lord of history, the master of man's actions, is, in a way, making him responsible for everything that happens. Naturally, we must make reservations, as Scripture does; the stories of the Creation and the Fall, for instance, clearly show that God is only responsible for the good things; sinful ones (even physical evils like bodily pain) cannot come from Yahweh; they have come into the world through sin, that is, through man. Nevertheless, this view is not always logically maintained; many expressions in the Old Testament make it look as if

Yahweh directly influences all human actions, including evil ones, in order that he may thus work out his plans. If this were so, not only would it affect human liberty, which is implicit in the Old Testament; it would also make Yahweh responsible for sin. There are many passages where Yahweh appears to be the instigator of evil deeds; he even seems to compel man to do wrong. Thus we read repeatedly in the stories preceding the Exodus that he hardened Pharaoh's heart so that he would not let the Israelites leave. (Exod. 9:1, 10:1, 20:27, 11:10, 14:8.) Pharaoh's refusal is attributed to Yahweh. Is this not a contradiction of Yahweh's sanctity? I certainly think so and, in my opinion, so did Israel in the fullness of her religious development. But it needed prolonged reflection before she could bring herself to weigh Yahweh's universal causality against man's responsibility for sin and evil. She noted that evil seemed to fit into Yahweh's plans; hence the unreserved application of the principle — which is in itself correct — that every occurrence originates in Yahweh and that, accordingly, he causes things to happen the way they do:

> Then the Lord said to Moses, "Go in to Pharaoh; for I have hardened his heart and the heart of his servants, that I may show these signs of mine among them, and that you may tell in the hearing of your son and of your son's son how I have made sport of the Egyptians and what signs I have done among them; that you may know that I am the Lord." [Exod. 10:1-2]

This is not a denial of human freedom, nor is it a negation of Yahweh's sanctity, and inability to cause any evil whatever; but because the matter has not been thought out systematically and God's qualities have not been weighed one against the other, certain essential nuances have been left out and the emphases have been placed too one-sidedly, and even incorrectly for the reader whose grasp is not very clear. In actual fact, what lies behind it all is a desire to demonstrate how seriously God's dominion over history is regarded.

The same conceptions are also found with other peoples of pre-Asiatic culture — at least, in principle. Though they have no historiography like Israel's, it is, nevertheless, a mark of their awareness of the gods that they attribute to them the events which can be held to be turning-points in history. The famous Moabite Stone of Mesha (about 830 BC) will serve as an example: "I am Mesha, son of Kemosh, king of Moab . . . I built this height for Kemosh in Qarloh . . . because he has delivered me from all kings and has made me look down on those who hated me . . ." It is obvious that these conceptions were given a special complexion in ancient Israel and became incorporated in Israel's religion.

3

THE LORD OF NATURE

Yahweh's activity is also revealed in nature. In many respects, present-day Christians see this in a different light from that of the Israelites of the Old Covenant. Quite a few, no doubt, consider the question of the relationship between God and nature adequately answered by the simple statement that God has created everything; but if their awareness of God goes no deeper than that, it is inferior to the consciousness of Old-Testament times. Yet it is hardly surprising that, for most of us, this should be the full extent of our awareness. In our time and age man has made so many discoveries about the laws of nature that he almost spontaneously regards God exclusively as the "originator," the Person who has set this beautiful and accurately running piece of machinery in motion. Indeed, we should have no difficulty in assuming even that everything functions without anyone's playing an "active" part. Although we are, of course aware — in theory at least — that God is active even in the smallest and least important of natural phenomena, nevertheless for many of us it has not grown into a lively awareness. We are so well informed on the causes behind changes in temperature, wind, rain, hail, storm and floods, sickness

and health, and even death, that we all too easily
forget that God is behind all these active causes.

If this is our frame of mind when we read the
books of the Old Testament, one of the first things
that strike us is the great number of "wonders" that
have taken place. We read, for instance, how
Yahweh divided the waters of the Red Sea to give
the Israelites safe passage and let them flow back
again to destroy the Egyptian armies; how, in the
desert, he sent manna and quails to feed them and
made water spring from the rock to quench their
thirst; and how he caused the walls of Jericho to
collapse and delivered the city into the hands of
Israel. Christians who read this often exclaim: "How
much everything has changed! Why doesn't God do
these things now? How people would believe in him!"

The question, however, is hardly whether God has
changed his line of action. Although this would not
be impossible, it seems more likely that it is we who
are altogether different. We are not in the habit of
noticing the wonders that are constantly taking place
within our reach because we often lose sight of the
fact that God is active in everything that happens.
When we speak of a wonder we mean something sen-
sational, something that cannot be given a natural
explanation, an occurrence that stumps everyone. And
if some scientific development shows us a natural
explanation for it, we feel disappointed, even cheated
and shaken in our belief. We are even apt to brand
as rationalists those who try to explain such wonders
naturally, instead of considering whether we have
not held wrong ideas on what constitutes a wonder.

Probably a far too apologetics-minded position has led us astray. For us a wonder is not so much a sign of God's activity in certain events as a happening which we can use to prove that God exists and intervenes in events. This is why we make certain demands on a wonder — a miracle; we demand that it should defy all natural explanation, even that we should be able to prove that natural explanations are impossible to find. What we forget is that this is a condition for the compelling power of a wonder, not for a wonder as such. By straining our apologetic position we have made a wonder into something that is different from what it was for the believer in the Old Testament — and, for that matter, in ancient Christendom — for we only speak of a wonder when we see the laws of nature opposed or temporarily suspended.

In the Old Testament a wonder means anything in which God's concern with man is made manifest, even when the phenomena follow definite laws. For the people of those times the daily rising and going down of the sun was as much a marvel of God's goodness as the occurrences which were specifically called wonders. The fact that every day anew God arranged events in such a way that they were in harmony with his plans, was another reason for ancient Israel to admire God's goodness. For the Israelites, wonders were, in the first place, marvels of God's providence. Even though they understood the natural causes which they saw him use, they could see no reason in this for denying their wonderful nature. If we read Pss. 14, 29, 135, and 136 we shall find proof of this.

Scripture itself clearly shows that this is the line to
follow; it is not an invention of the exegetes to get
themselves out of a tight corner. Nor should we consider such an interpretation to be a disfigurement of
Scripture, as doing away with the wonders in it.
Rather it teaches us to admire Scripture for bearing
witness to a profoundly religious view of things. Let
us take, for instance, the story of the passage through
the Red Sea, with which everyone is familiar. Many,
somewhat misled by the way in which they have once
heard it related, imagine this event as something
completely inexplicable. And they are on the whole
confirmed in their view by the usual illustrations:
the water standing upright like two steep and high
walls, leaving a narrow corridor through which the
children of Israel cross dry-footed whilst the armies
of Pharaoh, who have followed, are covered by the
waters and drowned. This is how Exodus describes it:

> Then Moses stretched out his hand over the sea; and the
> Lord drove the sea back by a strong east wind all night, and
> made the sea dry land, and the waters were divided. And
> the people of Israel went into the midst of the sea on dry
> ground, the waters being a wall to them on their right hand
> and on their left. [Exod. 14:21-22]

There is, indeed, mention of walls, but not high or
steep ones. Even for us, a wall still remains a symbol
of firmness and immobility; but what is far more important is that we should observe the way Yahweh
performed this wonder: by making a strong easterly
wind blow all night. I do not intend to labor this
point; I shall be content with pointing out that it is
at least plain from this instance that Yahweh, in his

wonders, does not go counter to the laws of nature
and that he is just as capable of performing them by
directing that the laws of nature shall work in a
certain way at any given moment. Does this make
it cease to be a wonder? Of course not, though the
apologetic value of such a wonder becomes at least
doubtful. Does not Yahweh, after all, have a hand
in everything that happens?

Many of the events related in the Old Testament
cannot be given such an explanation and they may,
therefore, be regarded as wonders in the apologetic
sense. But this is only a side-issue here; our present
concern is with ancient Israel's conviction that Yahweh
is active in nature, in all places and at all times —
even in those cases where the natural causes are
known. It is plain from this that in the Israelite's conception Yahweh does not merely manifest himself at
the beginning of creation, but reveals himself every
moment anew as the Lord of nature, because in her
he is active and finds the means to guide events in a
certain direction — in a conspicuous fashion or otherwise.

This awareness forms the background of many Old-
Testament stories, and some readers may regret the
fact that certain events can thus be reduced to normal proportions. In fact it is a gain; the wonders are
not reduced but rather increased since God is held
to be active in all things. And there is the further
gain that attention is diverted from the accidental and
concentrated on the important. Instead of admiring
God in visible facts we learn to admire his invisible
guidance in every occurrence. We learn to admire

the way God guided the religious conviction of his people — a way that really does him justice: he made them see that his omnipotence and providence are active at all times and in all places, and that he is ever concerned with his creation — especially with man.

4

THE GOD WHO SPEAKS

Finally, the living God reveals himself by his word. He makes his presence known, not only by what he does in history and in nature but also — and more especially — by what he says. This is of fundamental importance, for only a believer is aware of his presence and activity in nature and in history. What then, we may ask, is the real basis for belief in Yahweh? There can be only one answer: his own word. According to the religious conceptions of the ancient East, the world of the gods was not completely cut off from that of men. On the contrary, although these two worlds might appear detached from each other, they were connected all the same; inter-communication must, therefore, be practicable, and consequently it must be possible for the words of the gods to be heard on earth.

Ancient Israel, too, held this to be an evident possibility. Sometimes Yahweh even went so far as to show himself, but only on very rare occasions. We find descriptions of these appearances in a few sporadic stories and it is precisely their exceptional character and the restraint in their telling that warn us to take them seriously. Israelite tradition regards Moses as the man who was given the privilege of seeing Yahweh face to face. A word from Yahweh about him has survived: "With him I speak mouth to mouth, clearly, and not in dark speech; and he beholds the form of the Lord." (Num. 12:8) Was Moses really allowed to see Yahweh face to face? Other texts suggest he was not. In Exod. 33:18-23, we find an extensive description of the way Yahweh, at Moses' request, showed himself to him — but only from the back. In another place (Exod. 24:1-11) we read that Yahweh showed himself not only to Moses and Aaron but also to Nadab, Abihu and seventy of the elders of Israel. The emphasis in *v.* 11 on the statement that Yahweh did not lay his hand on them though they had seen him shows the reality of Yahweh's presence. Yahweh even appeared to the entire people, according to a tradition woven into Exod. 19:16-25, although there seems to be another version of the story (contained in the same verses) which denies it. Finally, we read in Gen. 32 about the mysterious struggle of Jacob, the founder of Israel, with a stranger who later turned out to be Yahweh — though it happens at night and darkness prevents Jacob from seeing much. This is how it always goes: we read of someone being allowed to see Yahweh but not what he looked like. At least one thing is obvious; Yahweh did on occasion visibly show himself, but nearly every time it was not so much the actual vision that mattered as some word that went with it.

Nearly all primitive religions made attempts to find out, by one means or another, what was the will of their god when there was some doubt about it, just as they also tried to find out how an undertaking was to end up. The way they set about consulting their

god was, usually, through the intervention of experts
who were able to read the god's reply in certain signs
and pass the message on. This was the practice also
in the pre-Asiatic culture's sphere of influence, and
Israel was no exception, as is borne out by the pro-
hibition of several methods for obtaining Yahweh's
answer:

"There shall not be found among you any one who burns
his son or his daughter as an offering, any one who practices
divination, a soothsayer, or an augur, or a sorcerer, or a
charmer, or a medium, or a wizard, or a necromancer."
[Deut. 28:10-11]

This precept was, nevertheless, broken, for instance
by Saul, who let the medium of Endor bring up the
spirit of the dead Samuel for questioning. (1 Sam.
28:3-25) Other methods for obtaining a decisive
answer from Yahweh were permitted and were indeed
customary in Israel, but they always had to be used
through the intervention of a priest or a generally
acknowledged prophet to make sure it really was
God's word that was heard. It seems that the question was always posed in such a way that the answer
could only be Yes or No. The priest or prophet was
able to find out God's decision — and pass it on to the
faithful — by drawing lots, by throwing arrows, from
the Urim and Thummim, from the ephod of the high
priest and through other signs. Similar practices seem
to have existed in New-Testament times; one thinks
of the choice of a substitute for Judas:

And they put forward two, Joseph called Barsabbas, who
was surnamed Justus, and Matthias. And they prayed and

said, "Lord, who knowest the hearts of all men, show which one of these two thou hast chosen to take the place in this ministry and apostleship from which Judas turned aside, to go to his own place." And they cast lots for them, and the lot fell on Matthias; and he was enrolled with the eleven apostles. [Acts 1:23-26]

Dreams were also regarded as media for hearing Yahweh's voice, just as the other inhabitants of the "fertile crescent" imagined they could hear their gods in them. Sometimes the meaning of such a dream was immediately obvious, as with Jacob's (Gen. 28:12-22); mostly it was hidden and only to be read by an expert, usually a priest or a prophet.

The normal way in which Yahweh's word came to the people was by the word of Prophets. In the golden age of Israel's religion prophecy achieved predominance and in this connection it is striking that, after the banning of the black magic already referred to, Israel was told how God's word was to be received:

The Lord your God will raise up for you a prophet like me [Moses] from among you, from your brethren — him you shall heed — just as you desired of the Lord your God at Horeb on the day of the assembly, when you said, "Let me not hear again the voice of the Lord my God, or see this great fire any more, lest I die." And the Lord said to me, "They have rightly said all that they have spoken. I will raise up for them a prophet like you from among their brethren; and I will put my words in his mouth, and he shall speak to them all that I command him." [Deut. 18:15-18]

For the people the prophet was the man who preached Yahweh's word and was sent by him to

speak of salvation and redemption, and particularly
to impress his commandments upon the people and
let them know their religious position. Originally prophetism seems to have been not so much an established institution as a phenomenon which occurred
whenever God's spirit promoted someone to speak his
word. This was often coupled with ecstatic condi-
tions. In a sense the Prophets can be compared with
the Judges, the saviours who, in the days of the kingdom, rose up here and there to bring a solution to
difficult situations, according to circumstances and
the way Yahweh's spirit prompted them. But there
is one difference that immediately catches the eye:
the prophet used only spiritual means, words and
symbols. His concern was Yahweh's word which he
spoke, the message of salvation (and sometimes
punishment) and the call to repentance.

Other peoples also knew such prophets and in
their actions they were reminiscent of the prophets
of Israel. Even now, in the Near East, we can see
people working themselves up, through music and
dancing, into ecstasies similar to those we read about
in connection with certain groups of prophets. These
were common phenomena, but behind their outward
similarities lay one great difference: only Yahweh's
prophets called to repentance, to a life of faithful
obedience to the law and response to Yahweh's plans,
and to an inner experience of the Covenant.

This distinguished them also from false prophets.
Prophetism seems, indeed, to have developed gradually into an officially recognized institution, as it did
elsewhere. Apart from the "freelance" prophets, there

were those who were tied to the Temple or the court. The court-prophets in particular were all too often intent on their personal wellbeing; they were dependent on the king, who could dismiss them when it pleased him — if he left it at that — and were, therefore always tempted to prophesy only what would be agreeable in official quarters. Thus it came about that the true prophets, for whom only the divine word of Yahweh was a norm, repeatedly clashed with them, especially when they prophesied punishment and disaster or made demands which official circles were not prepared to meet.

Anyway, the period in which we hear of Yahweh's prophets is not all that extensive. It is only in the age of Samuel that we do so, in other words, when the era of the Judges is past. And after the fifth century BC, Israel had no prophets at all. Later, wise men made their appearance to stress the old truths once again, but they do not seem to have been aware of any special vocation and even give the impression that they were rather ashamed they were not prophets. Indeed, they often published their books under a pseudonym, usually adopting the names of great figures from the past (The Wisdom of Solomon, The Psalms of Solomon etc.).

The heart of the prophetic message is always God's word. We frequently read in prophetic literature statements such as "Thus says the Lord" or "An oracle of the Lord." With what right does the prophet put forward his words as being God's? Or — to put it differently — what right had he to call himself a prophet? Obviously he could only proclaim as an ora-

cle what he himself had heard from Yahweh. Thus
we often read in the titles of the prophetic books,
"The word of the Lord which was addressed to . . ."
How the divine word came to them is not easy to
establish. Sometimes reference is made to a vision,
now and again to dreams, but mostly no further explanations are forthcoming. The prophet's knowledge
is not limited to the present; he also looks into the
past and the future; he is a seer, though prophesying
is not his chief preoccupation. When he predicts the
future he always does so to emphasize his preaching,
in an endeavor to persuade the unbelievers to accept
his word as being Yahweh's word which can either
make or break. Similarly, the word of the Prophets
is a strong phrase which, once spoken, never fails
in its effect. It is through the word of the Prophets
that Yahweh shows his faithfulness to Israel, handing
out reward and punishment or issuing threats and
promises in order to keep Israel on the narrow path
and persuade her to remain, of her own free will,
bound to him as his chosen people.

5

THE ONLY ONE

The Christian too is thoroughly convinced of the supremacy of God's reign, and this conviction is no doubt chiefly based on the authority of God's own revelation, although it usually bears very strong traces of philosophic thought. Reflection on what God is, necessarily leads him to the conclusion that there is only one God, and an analysis of the concept "God" makes him infer the absurdity of accepting several gods. Even if he is unable to draw this conclusion for himself, he has been clearly shown in his religious instruction the line he must follow to arrive at it. It would be silly to ignore its usefulness, but its danger should also be recognized. The abstract question of *What* God is does in practice become primary, and the question of *Who* God is becomes a secondary one. And it is often impossible to proceed from these abstractions to the reality of God, with the result that God becomes not a person but a remote power.

For ancient Israel too, belief in the one God, Yahweh, was primary, but she arrived at her conception by a different process, namely, through her immediate religious experience. Yahweh revealed himself to Israel as the only Lord of creation, claiming for himself the service of Israel and through her the whole of

humanity. But we should not imagine that the Israelite was able to grasp this reality all at once. Its content and depth were only gradually revealed; and
Israel was even slower in grasping and understanding
them. For us, who must rely on the details of Scripture for our participation in Israel's struggle, belief
in one God begins with the word Yahweh addressed
to Israel through Moses, his prophet: "I am the Lord
your God, who brought you out of the land of Egypt,
out of the house of bondage. You shall have no other
gods before me." (Exod. 20:2-3) Yahweh had already
revealed himself to Moses as the God of the forefathers (Exod. 3:6) and, according to tradition, he had
also spoken to the Patriarchs, but it was only now
that he made his claim on the people. Yahweh did
not tell them (yet) that the other peoples' gods were
not in fact gods at all. From the very beginning he
had been understood to be the greatest of all, and
also the greatest among gods (if such existed): "Who
is like thee, O Lord, among the Gods? Who is like
thee, majestic in holiness, terrible in glorious deeds,
doing wonders?" (Exod. 15:11)

Although Yahweh manifested himself as the God
of Israel, there are a number of indications from
which any clear-sighted person can understand the
universality of Yahweh's power. According to eastern
conceptions each people had one or more gods of
its own. In the minds of their worshippers their power
was, therefore, confined to that particular people and
thus territorially limited. The territory of a people
was the territory of its god of gods. Yahweh's chosen
people, however, had nothing and, though she had

been promised a country, Israel had little prospect of becoming a normal sedentary people within the foreseeable future. At that time she did not even have her own hunting-and-plundering-ground like other nomadic peoples. The fact that Yahweh chose this people suggests that the God of Israel was different from other peoples' gods and that his power knew neither territorial limits nor borders in space. Indeed, this is expressed in the adventures of the Chosen People: Yahweh manifests his power in Egypt, where he appears to reign over life and death, and nature behaves in accordance with his will. He shows the Egyptians and the children of Israel his "strong arm," or his power, as revealed in the wonders of Moses and in the punishments sent down on Egypt by Yahweh. His power is no less evident in the desert no-man's land, where he leads and helps the people and punishes it when necessary. And at the occupation of Canaan Yahweh shows that the gods who own that territory must give way to him. These are the experiences which led Israel to the conclusion that her God was mightier than the gods of other peoples.

It is striking in this connection that Israel's worship is offered to a God who is not only without his peer among the other gods but does not even permit his people to adore gods who are considered to be his subordinates. Nor should this be regarded as the normal run of things, for with Israel's neighbors it was altogether different. While it is true that there is usually a super-god, he has, as a rule, a goddess for his wife. Their divine marriage does not remain childless and their children, together with other gods

and sometimes demigods, become the faithful —
and, on occasion, faithless — servants of the super-
god, who exercises his dominion through them. In
this divine society not only quarrels and disunity but
divorce and unfaithfulness are accepted. In the religious experience of their worshippers a tutelary
deity sometimes occupies a much greater place than
the super-god. It is not surprising, then, that the
goddesses of fertility enjoyed a great following of
devoted admirers, although the fact that their cult
consisted of all manner of sexual debauches no doubt
had something to do with it too.

Yahweh, the God of Israel, on the contrary, is a
lonely God, sitting all by himself on his divine throne
in heaven, without consort or other gods. The Hebrew does not even have a word for "goddess."
Whereas the other peoples reduce the diversity of
phenomena to the existence of a collection of gods,
Israel reduces everything to Yahweh, who has revealed himself in such an overwhelming way that his
chosen ones feel there can be no place in their hearts
for anyone but him. Israel has never thought up a
kind of divine division of labor as a reflection in
heaven of human limitations on earth. Nor is there
a division of worship. Yahweh's only company is a
heavenly court of angels, messengers who maintain
direct contact with the world of man; but they always remain in an absolutely subordinate position,
and though they bathe in Yahweh's reflected glory,
it is never regarded as a reason for worshipping them,
however much respect the sight of such heavenly
messengers may command.

All this is really obvious to us and this is why we all too easily forget that in the pre-Asiatic culture it was something unique. Man had made himself gods in his own image, afflicted with human passions and defects of character; their power was limited and their superiority lay principally in the fact that they were above morality, which in fact meant that they were immoral. They were not even free from adversity and bad luck. We should do well to remember that the environment Abraham left behind when he set out from Haran was a pagan one. The roots of Israel's genealogical tree lying as they do in Mesopotamia, which had a well-filled pantheon, it goes without saying it needed the greatest effort and struggle to cut oneself off from it all. The fact that the people habitually lived in pagan surroundings did nothing to reduce these difficulties. This applied in the first place to Egypt: regret for the fleshpots of Egypt probably stands for more than just a minimum of material wellbeing. Later on, too, they maintained such close relations with their mighty neighbors that the Egyptian gods found worshippers even in Israel, as shown, among other texts, in Jer. 44. More dangerous still was the idolatry and the whole way of life which obtained in Canaan. It was not without reason that Yahweh had forbidden the people to maintain contact with the native population and had even ordered its eradication, but this did not prevent fertility goddesses from finding many worshippers among the Israelites.

In Canaan the worship of Yahweh seems to have taken place not only in the sanctuary which had been

brought along from the desert but also in the existing
temples. Although they still worshipped the same
God, the fact that these ancient temples were filled
with memories of other gods, offered at least an inducement for maintaining Yahweh's worship on the
right lines. Herein lies the great importance of David's
plan for the erection of one central and mighty temple — though, as it happened, only Solomon was able
to carry it out. Was this centralization ever fully
achieved? Everyone knows that one of Jeroboam's
first administrative acts after the partition of the
kingdom was the erection of two new sanctuaries, one
at Dan, the other at Bethel, where the cult was at
least orthodox. And the reform under the pious King
Josiah (639-609 BC) proves that, if the centralization
was ever completed, Judah had been quick to revert
to the old habits.

The influence of Assyria and Babylon produced
new dangers and one can imagine that during the
Babylonian exile the temptation proved too much for
many. After a period of relative respite during the
Persian era the danger was removed when the Hellen-
istic influence reached Judah; first the old customs
were renounced — following the usual pattern — and
later on Yahweh was held to be an antiquated God
who did not really fit in with the times.

So we see that Israel's belief in Yahweh was hardly
ever free from threats and grew and deepened despite
every oppression, perhaps even because of it. The sad
results of the excavations in Palestine prove how vul-
nerable the people were to temptation; idols from al-

most every period are found nearly everywhere, most
of them images of the fertility goddesses.

Often it was the kings — the anointed of Yahweh!
— who, by their own example, led the people in these
practices. One thinks of Solomon who, by his marriages to foreign princesses — with their own gods
and goddesses — showed that his wisdom was only
relative; or of King Ahab, in the Northern Kingdom,
who officially introduced the worship of Baal.

In such circumstances it was the Prophets who unceasingly fought for the honor of Yahweh, Elijah
being their most typical representative. (1 Kings
16:29ff) He never let up in his forceful opposition
to Ahab and his Tyrian wife and constantly appealed
to the people to remain faithful to Yahweh. As a
punishment for their defection he prophesied a terrible drought and, in consequence, famine. The high-
light of his mission was the sacrifice which he staged
on Mount Carmel. Both the priests of Baal and
Elijah himself were to prepare an offering, but the
god who set light to it was the one the people would
recognize as the true one. Baal's priests vainly made
grotesque efforts to move their god to light the offering and so prove his existence; but at Elijah's prayer
Yahweh kindled the offering prepared for him by the
prophet and showed the people that he was the one
who helped them. For, when they confessed: "The
Lord, he is God; the Lord, he is God" (1 Kings
18:39), and the prophets of Baal had been killed,
the heavens opened up and the long-expected rains
came down at last.

The prophets' care for Israel's faith only means,

on closer examination, that it was Yahweh himself
who was begging his people to remain faithful to him.
Yahweh had already revealed to Moses that he
demanded his people's undivided worship. Consequently, on Mount Sinai they were made to choose
whether or not they were prepared to recognize
Yahweh (Exod. 14:20); in the Covenant the choice
was made in Yahweh's favor (or rather, perhaps in
the people's!) (Exod. 24:1-11.) After the occupation
of Canaan, at the assembly in Shechem, the people
were again made to choose, this time by Joshua; again
they opted for the service of Yahweh (Joshua 24)
and again the Covenant was renewed. Whenever
Israel showed signs of losing sight of this revelation
of Yahweh and of forgetting that she had pledged
him her word, he sent prophets along to refresh her
memory.

When we try to sketch the development of Israel's
concepts, the thought which we find expressed in
Deut. 32 strikes us as being a particularly old one
and a direct reflection of the experience that Yahweh
always sustains and assists Israel:

When the Most High gave to the nations their inheritance,
when he separated the sons of men, he fixed the bounds of
the peoples according to the number of the sons of God. For
the Lord's portion in his people, Jacob his allotted heritage.
He found him in a desert land, and in the howling waste of
the wilderness; he encircled him, he cared for him, he kept
him as the apple of his eye . . . the Lord alone did lead him,
and there was no foreign god with him. [vv. 8-12]

We might understand this in the sense that the
"sons of God" (the angels) who are mentioned here

were originally the other gods who now have to be
satisfied with the other peoples' worship; this picture
has always been dear to Israel and we even come
across it in the fairly late Book of Daniel. (20:13;
20:20-21.) Israel's ability to grow into a great people
and take possession of the land — with Yahweh's
support, and in the face of every opposition — proves
that he is the greatest of the gods. This is frequently
celebrated in places such as the Psalms, for instance
in 95:3-5:

> For the Lord is a great God, and a great King above all
> gods. In his hand are the depths of the earth; the heights
> of the mountains are his also. The sea is his, for he made it;
> for his hands formed the dry land.

Even when Yahweh has come to be recognized as
the creator and governor of the whole universe, we
still find other gods mentioned. (See, for instance, Ps.
135:5; 138:1.) At the time when these psalms were
first sung, the real meaning of this mode of expression
was probably no longer consciously remembered;
but the very fact of its existence proves clearly that
there has certainly been a period when the conse-
quences of Yahweh's exclusive demand were not
properly appreciated and the gods of the other
peoples were held to be as real as Yahweh.

Indeed, several texts bear this out. In the Book of
Judges, for instance, we read that Jephtah sent a
message to the King of the Amorites regarding a
piece of land whose title was being contested:

> So then the Lord, the God of Israel, dispossessed the
> Amorites from his people Israel; and are you to take possession

of them? Will you not possess what Chemosh your god gives
you to possess? And all that the Lord our God has dispos-
sessed before us, we will possess.

We might be tempted to remark that this is not the
only place where Jephtah betrays a lack of proper
understanding of Yahweh's plans, or to explain that
he was only adapting himself to the views of the
opposition. But we find a passage from David in
which the same line of thought is evident; when
Saul drives him from the country, this is his reply:

Now therefore let my lord the king hear the words of his
servant. If it is the Lord who has stirred you up against me,
may he accept an offering; but if it is men, may they be
cursed before the Lord, for they have driven me out this
day that I should have no share in the heritage of the Lord,
saying, "Go, serve other gods."

For David, leaving the country obviously also means
entering into the territories of other gods. Even as
late as the eighth century we read in Micah — a
prophet, be it noted: "For all the peoples walk each
in the name of its god, but we will walk in the name
of the Lord our God for ever and ever." (4:5) The
phrase "our God," which we meet so often, seems to
have been used originally to distinguish the God of
Israel from other gods.

After all this there can, surely, be no further doubt
that ancient Israel made laborious efforts to acquire
the pure and perfect awareness of divine authority
vested exclusively in Yahweh. It was only by a long
purifying process that the hereditary taint of the pagan past was removed and it needed a constant strug-

gle to resist polytheism, which, in one form or
another, lay ever in wait at every turn of Israel's path
through the ages.

The word that finally set them free and showed the
other gods to be shams, figments in the imagination
of their worshippers, with no real existence, appears
to have been first uttered by Isaiah; he ripped the
mask from the idols that were worshipped on all
sides, and found nothing behind them:

> Thus says the Lord, the King of Israel and his Redeemer,
> the Lord of hosts: "I am the first and I am the last; besides
> me there is no god. Who is like me? Let him proclaim it,
> let him declare and set it forth before me. Who has an-
> nounced from of old the things to come? Let them tell us
> what is yet to be. Fear not, nor be afraid; have I not told
> you from of old and declared it? And you are my witnesses!
> Is there a God besides me? There is no Rock; I know not
> any." All who make idols are nothing, and the things they de-
> light in do not profit; their witnesses neither see nor know,
> that they may be put to shame. Who fashions a god or casts
> an image, that is profitable for nothing? Behold, all his fellows
> shall be put to shame, and the craftsmen are but men."
> [44:6-9; also the following verses; and more extensively in
> 41:21-29.]

In fact, he was already expressing in different words
what Paul was to write later: "They . . . exchanged
the glory of the immortal God for images resembling
mortal man or birds or animals or reptiles." (Rom.
1:23) Whereas Israel believed Yahweh to have
fashioned man in his image and likeness, the pagans
— literally understood — appear to have made gods
in their own image and likeness, even in that of

animals; a perversion in the real sense of the term.

The words of Isaiah, "idols are nothing," were passed on as a shout of triumph and we find them in Pss. 115 and 135, Hab. 2:18, and in Jer. 10 where we read:

> " 'The customs of the peoples are false. A tree from the forest is cut down, and worked with an axe by the hands of a craftsman. Men deck it with silver and gold; they fasten it with hammer and nails so that it cannot move. Their idols are like scarecrows in a cucumber field, and they cannot speak; they have to be carried, for they cannot walk. Be not afraid of them, for they cannot do evil, neither is it in them to do good.' There is none like thee, O Lord; thou art great, and thy name is great in might. Who would not fear thee, O King of the nations?" [vv. 3-7]

This passage shows great resemblance to Isa. 44:12ff. Later on the author of the Book of Wisdom also was to wield the weapon of mockery. (13:15)

The conclusion that the gods were nothing was, nevertheless, not the last word by any means. For, although the false gods were not real gods, they still retained a certain reality in so far as they opposed Yahweh, drew Israel away from him and kept the other peoples in fetters. This is shown, for instance, in that great hymn which Deut. 32 represents as a song of Moses and really needs to be read in its entirety for an appreciation of Israel's own conception of her struggle for a true awareness of God: "They stirred him [Yahweh] to jealousy with strange gods; with abominable practices they provoked him to anger. They sacrificed to demons which were no gods, to gods they had never known . . ." (vv. 16-17.)

This thought too seems to have been kept alive, for we still come across it in Paul, where he speaks about participation in pagan sacrifices and forbids the Christians to take part in them, for the following reasons:

Are not those who eat the sacrifices partners in the altar? What do I imply then? That food offered to idols is anything, or that an idol is anything? No, I imply that what pagans sacrifice they offer to demons and not to God. I do not want you to be partners with demons." [1 Cor. 10:19-20]

It is plain from all this that the confession of faith, in Deut. 6:4, which is daily repeated by religious Jews, is the culmination of a lengthy development, or rather, a protracted religious crisis. Already in Moses' time Yahweh had ordained that Israel should worship no other gods besides him, but it is only in Deuteronomy that Israel gives her answer; not just a theoretical one or a mere formulation of abstract truth, but a personal confession to Yahweh, who at last receives his due place in Israel's religious life: "Hear, O Israel: The Lord our God is one Lord; and you shall love the Lord your God with all your heart, and with all your soul, and with all your might." (Deut. 6:4-5) In the meantime Yahweh's mercies have been felt in such an overwhelming way that no other conclusion is possible:

The Lord alone did lead him, and there was no foreign god with him. He made him ride on the high places of the earth, and he ate the produce of the field; and he made him suck honey out of the rock, and oil out of the flinty rock . . . See now that I, even I, am he, and there is no god beside me;

I kill and I make alive; I wound and I heal; and there is none that can deliver out of my hand." [Deut. 32:12-13; 39; see also the song of David in 2 Sam. 22:32ff]

Ancient Israel was not to keep this conviction to herself; or — to put it more strongly — Yahweh gave her this conviction, not only for herself but as a gift to be handed down to all peoples. Ancient Israel was chosen from among all peoples but, at the same time, for all peoples. For Yahweh is the only God of the whole earth. When this conviction reached maturity, the conclusion suggested itself: All must worship him and Yahweh's name must be known all over the earth through Israel's witness. Again it was Isaiah who first stressed this: "I am the Lord, and there is no other, besides me there is no God; I gird you, though you do not know me, that men may know, from the rising of the sun and from the west, that there is none besides me." (45:5-6) And from the Psalms we can gather how the religious Jews adopted these thoughts of the prophet: "There is none like thee among the gods, O Lord, nor are there any works like thine. All the nations thou hast made shall come and bow down before thee, O Lord, and shall glorify thy name. For thou art great and doest wondrous things, thou alone art God." (Ps. 86:8-10)

6

EXALTED AND NEAR

The religious conviction that Yahweh is the only true God was not the only feature that distinguished Israel's awareness of God, when it had come to its full development, from that of her neighbors; perhaps not even the main one. For it seems likely that the awareness of Yahweh's immeasurable exaltation and, at the same time, inconceivable nearness, was much more fundamental; certainly it led to a deeper understanding of Yahweh's identity. The mere conviction that Yahweh alone is God, produced a certain amount of tension, because there was such a diversity and profuseness in the phenomena which the Israelites could observe — indeed, this is what led some religions to infer the existence of many gods. But the tension resulting from the awareness of Yahweh's exaltation and nearness was far greater, since the slightest exaggeration one way or the other was bound to bring confusion to their awareness of God.

It is often suggested that the ancient Israelite's veneration for Yahweh was founded solely on a deep respect — because he only saw the distance separating him from his God — and that, after the New Testament had bridged this gulf, the religious attitude which started as fear of the Lord developed into an all-encompassing love. This is a fair enough picture,

but its coloring has far more nuances than is often
imagined. Even the Old Testament knew very well
that man is not only separated from Yahweh by an
immeasurable distance but, at the same time, bound
to him by exceptionally intimate ties. And the Christian who has listened attentively to Jesus' words and
the reflections of the first generation of Christians is
thoroughly aware that the fear of the Lord is by no
means a thing of the past.

The vigor with which the books of the Old Testament give expression to the conviction of Yahweh's
exaltation is striking indeed. This can, of course, be
illustrated with quotations from isolated texts, such
as, for instance, Isa. 55:8-9: "For my thoughts are not
your thoughts, neither are your ways my ways, says
the Lord. For as the heavens are higher than the
earth, so are my ways higher than your ways and my
thoughts than your thoughts"; or Ps. 113:4-6: "The
Lord is high above all nations, and his glory above
the heavens! Who is like the Lord our God, who is
seated on high, who looks far down upon the heavens
and the earth?" But it is better to point out that the
Old Testament as a whole is filled with respect and
even fear of Yahweh.

Israel expresses the essence of Yahweh's exaltation
in the word "holy," viewed, however, against a different background from our own. A Christian who
speaks of holiness thinks, in the first place, of holy
persons, people who have led lives which were pleasing to God. His thoughts probably also go to objects
that have been admitted to the sphere of holiness
because they have been blessed or consecrated. But

in this connection we too easily forget that persons and objects are only called holy in a metaphorical sense. This is understandable, for we are in the habit of calling God by human names and using all sorts of human terms to express our conception of who he is. It is obvious, therefore, that we also mean to apply the word "holy" to him in the same way. But it is precisely the reverse: God is really absolute holiness. When we call a man holy, we use the term in a relative sense; when the Israelite calls God "the Holy One," it is an absolute pronouncement which can only be applied to Yahweh in the real sense of the word. And if he is holy, it is precisely because he is different from all else: "I am God and not man, the Holy One in your midst." (Hos. 11:9) "The Holy One of Israel" — as Isaiah so often calls Yahweh — is for the Israelite the inscrutable, incomprehensible, awe-inspiring (Deut. 10:17; 25:58; Ps. 47:5; 68:36, etc.) whom even the highest heavens cannot contain. (1 Kings 13:27) Holiness here is not, therefore, a moral category; it would be stupid to say that Yahweh leads a holy life. The authors of the Old Testament use the term "holy" primarily to indicate a sphere, defined by the presence of the Holy One, Yahweh, in which — in the general consensus of opinion — no man can bear to stay: "Who is able to stand before the Lord, this holy God?" (1 Sam. 6:20)

The definition of this sphere is reflected in the layout of the temple area. Herod's — and Solomon's, for that matter — has as its center the Holy of Holies (really a far too literal equivalent for "the most holy"); the place where Yahweh is present among his people and no one may enter save the high priest, once a year. In front of it is the sanctuary where only the priests have access. Before that and in the open is the forecourt of the priests with the altar for the burnt offerings, a small section of this inner court being accessible to all the Israelites. On the far side of a gated wall lies the Court of Women, again completely fenced in. Finally there is the great square which is open to all — and for that reason known as the Court of Gentiles — though the part directly adjoining the buildings is also surrounded with a low wall whose every opening bears a notice denying entry to non-Jews. Thus, the closer to Yahweh's presence, the holier the place and the greater the degree of holiness required from those who enter: Israelites, priests and high priests.

The thought of Yahweh's exceeding holiness plays an important part in the vision of Isaiah's calling:

In the year that King Uzziah died I saw the Lord sitting upon a throne, high and lifted up; and his train filled the temple. Above him stood the seraphim; each had six wings: with two he covered his face, and with two he covered his feet, and with two he flew. And one called to another and said: "Holy, holy, holy is the Lord of hosts; the whole earth is full of his glory." And the foundations of the thresholds shook at the voice of him who called, and the house was filled with smoke. [Is. 6:1-4]

In heaven also — which here lies in the same perspective as the temple — Yahweh is utterly and completely the Holy One. Even the seraphim are unable to bear his presence; they cover their face with their wings so that they should not see him, while two

other wings protect their "body" from Yahweh's an-
nihilating and crushing presence.

This brings us to a second consideration, which is
a corollary to the previous one: If Yahweh is so holy
that no man can bear his presence, it really must be
awesome. It is hardly surprising, then, that Isaiah,
seeing this vision, exclaimed: "Woe is me! For I am
lost; for I am a man of unclean lips, and I dwell in
the midst of a people of unclean lips; for my eyes
have seen the King, the Lord of hosts!" (Isa. 6:5)
Isaiah considered himself unclean because of his own
sins and those of his people. Uncleanness here is
the exact opposite of holiness; and this makes it
easier for us to understand why ancient Israel put so
much store by her purity laws. We often do not know
the exact reason for holding certain objects and actions unclean; what is certain is that contact with
them placed man in a sphere which was the very
opposite of Yahweh's, Israel's Holy One. But whenever someone saw Yahweh, the meeting seemed awesome to him; God's greatness was thought to pre-
clude all contact with him. When Abraham spoke
with God (or was it perhaps only with an angel —
who shall say?) he said explicitly: "Behold, I have
taken upon myself to speak to the Lord, I who am
but dust and ashes." (Gen. 18:27) And when Jacob,
in a dream at Bethel, had seen the angels of God
climbing up and down the ladder leading to heaven
and had, moreover, heard Yahweh's own voice, he
awoke in the grip of a mighty fear:

Then Jacob awoke from his sleep and said, "Surely the
Lord is in this place; and I did not know it." And he was

afraid, and said, "How awesome is this place! This is none
other than the house of God, and this is the gate of heaven."
[Gen. 28:16-17]

The fear of the Lord naturally promoted the view
that no one could behold Yahweh with impunity as
his greatness was so awe-inspiring that merely to
look upon him would blind a man and even make
him drop dead. Thus, when Yahweh appeared to
Moses in the desert and the latter found out who
was really speaking to him: "Moses hid his face,
for he was afraid to look at God." (Exod. 3:6) But
later Moses mustered enough courage to ask if he
might be allowed to see Yahweh:

"I pray thee, show me thy glory." And he [Yahweh] said,
"I will make all my goodness pass before you, and will proclaim before you my name 'The Lord'; and I will be gracious
to whom I will be gracious, and will show mercy on whom
I will show mercy." "But," he said, "you cannot see my face;
for man shall not see me and live." And the Lord said,
"Behold, there is a place by me where you shall stand upon
the rock; and while my glory passes by I will put you in a
cleft of the rock, and I will cover you with my hand until I
have passed by; then I will take away my hand, and you
shall see my back; but my face shall not be seen." [Exod.
33:18-23]

It is moving to see how God adapted himself to
these notions. And if even someone like Moses — and
later on an eminent man like Isaiah — was filled with
such a fear of Yahweh, it is obvious that this notion
was still stronger in the mass of the people. When all
was arranged for proclaiming the Law on Mount
Sinai and the air was filled with the noise of thunder
and the flashes of lightning, such a fear gripped the

people that they trembled and asked Moses: "You speak to us, and we will hear; but let not God speak to us, lest we die." (Exod. 20:19)

In Israel's hymnal too the thought of Yahweh's "awful" presence lives on in many songs.

The well-nigh immeasurable respect for Yahweh's holiness helps us to understand a number of passages from Scripture which might otherwise seem puzzling; read against this background they appear in a different light. When I discussed the layout of the temple buildings I noted that behind it lay the notion that not everyone was equally competent to come into contact with Yahweh. Anyone who touched the Holy One or even something belonging to his sphere of holiness without the required fitness to do so would be severely punished — no matter how good his intentions. We think, for instance, of the story of Uzzah:

And they carried the ark of God upon a new cart, and brought it out of the house of Abinadab which was on the hill; and Uzzah and Ahio, the sons of Abinadab, were driving the new cart with the ark of God . . . And when they came to the threshing floor of Nacon, Uzzah put out his hand to the ark of God and took hold of it, for the oxen stumbled. And the anger of the Lord was kindled against Uzzah; and God smote him there because he put forth his hand to the ark and he died there beside the ark of God. [2 Sam. 6:3-7]

If we consider the bare facts — detached from their interpretation — it looks as if Uzzah lost his life while trying to save the Ark from an accident. In the interpretation two things are of particular interest: First, the author is only mildly concerned with Uzzah's good intentions; he only mentions in passing that he was trying to prevent the Ark from toppling over. Second: Uzzah's death is thought to be due to the fact that he touched the Ark, despite his unfitness to do so. He touched the sphere of what was holy and divine and, in the opinion of ancient Israel, this is what caused his death. As we read this we should not ask ourselves in amazement how it is possible for God to punish someone's good intentions; the most we may do is to show surprise at the consistency of Israel's notions which made these people interpret the accident in this way.

The awareness of Yahweh's absolute sovereignty, his inviolability, his utter transcendence, his complete difference, his exaltation above everything and everyone, is certainly one of the basic motives of the Old Testament. And it is by no means an accident that man's sin is regarded primarily as an act in which man reaches up to God's unattainable level. Adam and Eve ate from the forbidden fruit because they thought it would make them like God: "The serpent said to the woman, 'You will not die. For God knows that when you eat of it your eyes will be opened, and you will be like God, knowing good and evil.'" (Gen. 3:4) Of course this may well start a discussion on what precisely is meant by "knowing good and evil"; but what is of greater importance according to the inspired author — who is really thinking along the line of Israel's holiest traditions — is that sin is nothing less than an attempt to bridge the distance between God and man and to place oneself on the same level as Yahweh. Indeed, in these words he exposes the very essence of every sin. The story of

the Tower of Babel seems to be an expression of the
same notion; the interpretation of the intentions of
those who built the tower runs on the same lines:
"They said to one another, 'Come, let us make bricks,
and burn them thoroughly . . .' They then said,
'Come, let us build ourselves a city, and a tower
with its top in the heavens . . .'" (Gen. 11:3-4) Of
course this can be regarded as no more than a graphic
description of the great height of the tower, but
Yahweh's reaction — as interpreted by the story — is
based on this thought: "Nothing that they propose
to do will now be impossible for them." (Gen. 11:6)
It seems probable, therefore, that Israelite tradition
saw this gigantic effort as an act of human presumption that tried to bridge the distance between the
world of man and that of God.

In any event, it is abundantly clear — to me, at
least — that, although the fear of the Lord is such
an important element in the Old Testament, there
is nevertheless, no justification for thinking chiefly of
Yahweh's chastening hand, ever ready to pounce
on the slightest deviation from his law. On the contrary, the fear of the Lord is far more closely bound
up with deep awareness that Yahweh's holiness is
so great that it simply consumes any man who is
bold enough to come too near. It has certainly not
been easy to keep this awareness of the infinite distance between Yahweh and man unsullied, for the
idolatry which unceasingly threatened Israel was —
in the manner of its incidence — another way of
bridging the distance between God and man; worshipping idols made the gods appear in human form.

God's excellence can, however, be over-emphasized by making out not only that man is unable to close the gap by throwing a bridge from his end, but that God cannot bridge it either, or at any rate does not do so. This is, in fact, the position of deism, which isolates God in heaven and man on earth without any active relations between them; a danger that ancient Israel never fell victim to. No other religion stresses the distance as much as the Israelite's, nor is there a religion in which God maintains such intimate relations with man. Emphasizing Yahweh's utter difference shows him at his true worth; emphasizing man's sinfulness stresses his complete worthlessness. But there comes an end to this worthlessness, for Yahweh is concerned for man's fate. Though all human efforts to penetrate right into heaven were bound to fail and end up in new sins, the matter did not rest there, for if we read on in the story of the Fall we see how Yahweh himself takes the initiative: he walks into the garden and asks Adam: "Where are you?" (Gen. 3:9) We see time after time in the Old Testament that God goes looking for man, visits him, speaks with him and lays himself bare — if this is not too profane an expression. God pursues him with his kindness, his benefactions and his mercy. When Yahweh wants to destroy the earth he first gets in touch with Noah; we read how he approaches the Patriarchs; in Israel's dire distress in Egypt he is the one who takes the initiative in her deliverance and liberation. Later he repeatedly addresses the people through the Prophets and on Mount Sinai he says to Moses: "The Lord, the Lord, a God merciful

and gracious, slow to anger, and abounding in steadfast love and faithfulness, keeping steadfast love for
thousands, forgiving iniquity and transgression and
sin, but who will by no means clear the guilty, visiting the iniquity of the fathers upon the children . . ."
(Exod. 34:6-7) Yahweh is, therefore, also a near
God; so near that he does not hesitate to call ancient
Israel his offspring and consider himself the Father
of his people.

In one of the most precious heirlooms which
Christendom has inherited from ancient Israel, the
Psalms, we frequently come across songs of praise
which bear witness to Israel's awareness of Yahweh's
intimate ties with his people and show us how God's
loving and watchful nearness is as keenly appreciated
as the infinite distance that separates man from God.
Ps. 103 should really be read in its entirety, but a few
verses at least must be quoted because they graphic-
ally express this intimacy in terms of the infinite
distance:

> For as the heavens are high above the earth, so great is
> his steadfast love toward those who fear him; as far as the
> east is from the west, so far does he remove our transgres-
> sions from us. As a father pities his children, so the Lord
> pities those who fear him. For he knows our frame; he
> remembers that we are dust. [Ps. 103:11-14]

It is not surprising, in this connection, that the
Prophets — under the inspiration of Yahweh's spirit
— borrowed images from the most intimate of human
relationships to express the relationship between
Yahweh and his people: "Can a woman forget her

sucking child, that she should have no compassion on
the son of her womb? Even these may forget, yet I
will not forget you." (Isa. 49:15; 66:13; Ps. 27:10)
But not only do they compare Yahweh's love to a
mother's; they are not ashamed to go further still and
take the example of married life. The frankest and
most beautiful interpretation of this point is found in
Ezekiel's sixteenth chapter; though perhaps rather
crude for our liking, it is, nevertheless, an exquisite
expression of Yahweh's love for ancient Israel. The
Old-Testament books often embroider on this metaphorical language; we should realize that we have
here gone to the very heart of the Old Testament:
God the Most Holy, the awe-inspiring One, before
whom no man can stand, condescends to make the
most intimate contact with his chosen ones.

Thus we see that the Most Holy does not leave the
profane world and sinful man to their fate. It is
really as Jacob saw it in his vision at Bethel: there
really is a ladder between heaven and earth and,
though Yahweh, the Most Holy, is infinitely exalted
above man, he has, nevertheless, walked into the
midst of humanity: "I am God and not man, the Holy
One in your midst." (Hos. 11:9) And though this has
come to pass in an undreamt-of fashion in the Old
Testament, Yahweh is present just the same among
his people in the New Testament.

7

THE RIGHTEOUS JUDGE

When we speak of God's justice, one of our first thoughts is that God wrongs no one and gives everyone his due. We are, in this respect, like children gathered round a huge birthday cake to see if anyone is getting too big a share. The thought that God rewards good and punishes evil is an immediate corollary, for these two different associations of ideas have a common basis: both are most important cases calling for the application of definite rules. And the "fair play" we demand from each other is also expected from God. Nor is it exceptional for us to meet people who can hardly hide their disapproval when — as so often happens — God does not appear to give equal shares to all; a common reaction in us humans. The Old Testament too not only speaks of a "jealous God" who does not allow his people to give their affection to false gods; it also mentions quite a number of jealous men who cannot bear God to give more to others than to themselves, especially when the others live less pious lives.

The awareness of Yahweh's justice has its roots in the fact that Yahweh is a judge. There is in this a direct connection with his kingship over Israel, for the ancient East, after all, knew no division of the

legislative, executive and judicial powers; all three
lay in the hands of one person, the king, who often
administered justice himself. Before the age of the
Kings, the highest judicial power was probably
vested in the tribal heads, who settled disputes and
tried to solve their fellow tribesmen's differences of
opinion, probably only achieving success after almost
endless negotiations, interrogations and pleadings
based on ancient tribal traditions. That the Kings
continued this practice, is borne out by the almost
legendary fame of a man like Solomon who is generally praised for his special wisdom — occasionally
even ingenuity — in reaching a solution. We need
only refer briefly to the graphic story of the two
women who fought before the judgment seat for
possession of a child. (1 Kings 3:16-28)

The quality most appreciated in a judge is integ-
rity, justice, incorruptibility; which, in fact, only
means that, whatever the circumstances, he never
deviates from the accepted standard of justice and
is, moreover, sharp-witted enough to detect cheating
in one of the litigating parties. Justice need not mean
that he must lead an impeccable life but rather
that he is beyond reproach in upholding the Law;
and this he never does in general, but always in particular cases submitted to him.

The first and real meaning of the term "justice" is,
therefore, bound up with the administration of justice. Thus it is that Yahweh is regarded as the righteous judge without a peer, who always rewards good
and punishes evil. This is the picture we see of him
from the first page of Scripture, at the same time be-

ing made aware that he is not only the righteous but
also the merciful judge who time and again takes
pity on man — especially on ancient Israel, even when
she is in the wrong. Here we should recall not only
the story of the Fall but others also, such as that of
the Flood, which brings out this very thought with
particular force. Yahweh's justice is sung in various
passages from the Psalms (for instance Ps. 7:7-18);
indeed, the thought that Yahweh is the righteous one
par excellence has influenced a whole tradition
which has made it into one of its motive forces. It
is very firmly established in Deuteronomy and has
exerted great influence on Joshua, Judges and the
books of Samuel and Kings.

Here then we find a notion of justice which, however different from our own, seems fundamental to
the Israelite of the Old Testament. Deuteronomy
clearly teaches us its principle: the guiding rules of
Yahweh's actions. These we see expressed in many
passages, perhaps in none more extensively than in
Chapter 28, which takes no less than fourteen verses
to list Yahweh's blessings on his people if it remains
faithful to his law, and devotes as many as fifty-five
verses to the disasters which will follow its desertion.

"And if you obey the voice of the Lord your God, being
careful to do all his commandments which I command you
this day, the Lord your God will set you high above all the
nations of the earth. And all the blessings shall come upon
you and overtake you, if you obey the voice of the Lord
your God . . . The Lord will cause your enemies who rise
against you to be defeated before you; they shall come out
against you one way, and flee before you seven ways . . .

And all the peoples of the earth shall see that you are called
by the name of the Lord; and they shall be afraid of you
. . . But if you will not obey the voice of the Lord your God
or be careful to do all his commandments and his statutes
which I command you this day, then all these curses shall
come upon you and overtake you . . . The Lord will cause
you to be defeated before your enemies; you shall go out
one way against them, and flee seven ways before them; and
you shall be a horror to all the kingdoms of the earth. [Deut.
28:1-2, 7, 10, 15, 25]

All prosperity is regarded as a reward from God, all
adversity as punishment.

Not only the books of Joshua and Judges, but also
— though in a lesser measure — those of Samuel and
Kings have been built on this simple, even oversim-
plified, plan. A few instances chosen at random will
illustrate this:

And the people of Israel did what was evil in the sight of
the Lord, forgetting the Lord their God, and serving the
Baals and the Asheroth. Therefore the anger of the Lord was
kindled against Israel, and he sold them into the hand of
Cushan-rishathaim king of Mesopotamia; and the people of
Israel served Cushan-rishathaim eight years. But when the
people of Israel cried to the Lord, the Lord raised up a
deliverer for the people of Israel, who delivered them,
Othniel the son of Kenaz, Caleb's younger brother. The
Spirit of the Lord came upon him, and he judged Israel; he
went out to war, and the Lord gave Cushan-rishathaim king
of Mesopotamia into his hand; and his hand prevailed over
Cushan-rishathaim. [Judges 3:7-10]

In the twenty-third year of Joash the son of Ahaziah, king
of Judah, Jehoahaz the son of Jehu began to reign over
Israel in Samaria, and he reigned seventeen years. He did

what was evil in the sight of the Lord, and followed the
sins of Jeroboam the son of Nebat, which he made Israel
to sin [namely, contention in public worship and the resultant
lapse into idolatry]; he did not depart from them. And the
anger of the Lord was kindled against Israel, and he gave
them continually into the hand of Hazael king of Syria and
into the hand of Ben-hadad the son of Hazael. Then Jehoahaz
besought the Lord, and the Lord hearkened to him; for he
saw the oppression of Israel, how the king of Syria oppressed
them. (Therefore the Lord gave Israel a saviour, so that they
escaped from the hand of the Syrians; and the people of
Israel dwelt in their homes as formerly.) [2 Kings 13:1-5]

Yahweh's justice shows up in two ways: first, he is
the one who rewards good and punishes evil; all
blessing and prosperity is a reward from Yahweh, all
adversity a punishment. Second, he faithfully keeps
to his own rules. Thus it is plain that in the Israelite's
conception, justice and faithfulness are connected.
Basically this faithfulness is founded on the covenant
Yahweh has made with Israel. But whilst he is faithful, he is — in the Israelite view — also a judge. His
faithfulness to Israel — which makes her conquer
other peoples and take possession of the Promised
Land — is also seen as a judgment on these peoples
and on the gods they worship. It is a condemnation
of them, sometimes even a death sentence, when
Yahweh orders Israel to wipe out the inhabitants of
a certain place. As for Israel, she emerges from the
proceedings in triumph, fully justified. But this
judgment of Yahweh is by no means an automatic
action, as witness the fact that it always goes against
Israel when her godless behavior puts her on the
side of the pagans; then Israel, like the others, falls

a victim to Yahweh's judgment. His justice demands
that in those circumstances even his chosen people
be condemned, and this does, in fact, happen frequently. Only when it repents and turns back to him
does Yahweh again impart his blessing. Thus he follows his own directions in the administration of justice without the slightest deviation.

It is obvious that there is something primitive in
the elaboration of these views. Present-day facts, indeed, clearly show that prosperity and a way of life
which hardly evokes the admiration of the faithful
often go together. Could things have been different
in Old Testament times? They have this appearance,
certainly, but no more than that. Other sources tell
us, for instance that King Omri's reign was a period
of prosperity and diplomatic successes, but we hardly
learn anything about his successes from the Books of
Kings. We are told in 1 Kings 16:21-28 that Omri built
himself a new capital, Samaria, but apart from that
he is — in company with the other kings of the
Northern Kingdom — classed with those who do evil
in the eyes of Yahweh. Is, then, the author misleading
his readers? Not at all, for those who are interested
in the facts themselves, are always referred to the
court chronicles: "Now the rest of the acts of Omri
which he did, and the might that he showed, are
they not written in the Book of the Chronicles of the
Kings of Israel?"(16:27; we should be careful not to
confuse this book with the Books of the Chronicles
which we are familiar with.) Unfortunately we do
not possess this book, but the author's procedure
shows that he is not concerned with facts as such but

with the lessons that can be learned from them, and that he only mentions them insofar as these lessons are made clearer by the relation of the facts.

What is primitive in this view is the thought that it is always on earth and in the course of history tha' Yahweh manifests his justice. For centuries Israel's vision was confined by matters earthly and temporal and, furthermore, there was originally a rather one-sided admiration of the way God always did justice to his people, with only scant attention paid to the fact that Yahweh also repaid the good and evil of individuals. We can appreciate this if we bear in mind that all the members of the Israelite community felt strongly linked by the bond of their common fate, a link that was not confined to the living generation but also bound the various generations together. For the Israelite, therefore, it almost went without saying that the sin of the individual was punished in all those who were bound to him, just as a blessing on one covered all his race. We find examples of this on almost every page of the historical books and see its principle formulated, for instance, in Exod. 20:5: "I the Lord your God am a jealous God, visiting the iniquity of the fathers upon the children to the third and the fourth generation of those who hate me, but showing steadfast love to thousands of those who love me and keep my commandments."

In the very first pages of Scripture, in the story of the Fall, we see this principle applied: because of the sin of one, all are punished, while the promised salvation will also benefit the whole community. It seems plain to me that this is a reality, not to be

pushed aside with the reflection that these are very
primitive notions brought back to life in later ages.
More than ever before, indeed, modern science shows
us that the faults and the qualities of the forebears
do live on in the living race. At most we can ask ourselves to what extent this phenomenon is of a moral
and not a physical or psychic order, and in how far
it can be regarded as a punishment properly speaking.
In any case, we cannot deny the saying which Jeremiah quotes every ground of truth: "The fathers
have eaten sour grapes, and the children's teeth are
set on edge." (Jer. 31:29) For that matter Jeremiah
himself amends the saying: "But every one shall die
for his own sin; each man who eats sour grapes, his
teeth shall be set on edge." (31:30) This is perfectly
true; the faults of the forebearers can reduce our
guilt, but where there is actual guilt, the culprit himself will have to bear the punishment. Man, however,
is never alone before Yahweh's judgment seat;
others are involved in his misdeeds and he himself
is not altogether innocent of the sins of others. But
that does not mean that all should, in consequence,
receive equal punishment. The troubled and turbid
situation which no one can unravel is plain enough
to God's eye. He, and only he, can weigh the responsibility of each and thus reward or punish according to one's deserts.

The other problem is a stickier one. As long as God's
reward and punishment are thought to be meted out
during man's lifetime and in this world, the facts
seem to be sadly at variance with this belief. Especially those who are rather lax appear to do well. How

does this tally? Ecclesiastes puts it pithily and free from the bitterness which is felt behind some of the Psalms: "In my vain life I have seen everything; there is a righteous man who perishes in his righteousness, and there is a wicked man who prolongs his life in his evil-doing." (7:15) Jeremiah himself had felt this problem to his cost, as well as several psalmists who, generally speaking, have no positive solution to suggest and merely stress that the sinner will not profit from his riches because he too must die. (Ps. 49) The author of Ps. 73 goes deeper; whilst noting that the sinners have a bad time when their end approaches, he seems aware that they have forfeited what is, after all, the most important of all: being with Yahweh.

No other passage makes us feel this problem as deeply as the Book of Job which is built entirely around the question why the righteous must suffer. The reader is not really offered a solution but is emphatically referred to God who knows what he is doing and does everything to a purpose, though man cannot see it.

The real solution was a long time coming and it was only recognized as such when Jewish-Semitic thought came under the fruitful influence of Greek philosophy. This brought along the first indication that there was quite possibly a real continuation of life after death; a new kind of life which was the very opposite of the languishing existence led by the "shades" in the realm of the dead, according to ancient Semitic conception. Actually this in itself gives the solution, for if all is not finished with man

when he dies it may well be possible that God only
repays him according to his merits after death. This
is not the place for us to study the development of
this new conception nor is it easy to establish when
it came to be commonly held by the masses. What
we do know is that in Dan. 12:2-3 it is no longer presented as a new idea:

And many of those who sleep in the dust of the earth
shall awake, some to everlasting life, and some to shame and
everlasting contempt. And those who are wise shall shine
like the brightness of the firmament; and those who turn
many to righteousness, like the stars for ever and ever.

It is clear, however, that this new conception is
closely related to the belief in the resurrection of the
dead (which probably made its definite breakthrough
in the Greek-Hellenistic period). That is how it is,
for instance, in the opening chapters of the Book of
Wisdom with their notable feeling of triumph — and
understandably so! For centuries the godly man had
been asking what was the good of his piety if the
sinner fared better than himself. Now he knew that
what he previously regarded as the end of the road
was really a new beginning.

One thing is certain: whatever else may have been
in doubt, Yahweh's justice never was. This is tacitly
held as an indisputable axiom. And this distinguishes
Israel's awareness of God in a very special way from
that of her neighbors, whose gods are often no more
than mighty despots imposing their will on all to no
purpose but their own satisfaction.

For the pious Israelite Yahweh's presence is always

a judiciary presence; none of man's actions escapes
him; he reads every intention and forthwith judges it.
In this connection it may well be illuminating that
— according to later rabbinical conception — even
Yahweh rests on the Sabbath without, however, al-
lowing it to interfere with the exercise of his judicial
powers.

8

GOD'S CHOSEN PEOPLE

Awareness of God is also awareness of self, and with Israel it is perhaps stronger and deeper-seated than with other peoples. She is profoundly convinced that she is Yahweh's own people, chosen by him from all the peoples of the world, and this conviction has probably been held from the earliest moments of her existence. It is notable and indeed very remarkable that we can find no attempt in the Old Testament to link Israel's election with any particular moment in her history, thus marking it as an event that took place at a well-defined moment in time. Some events, of course, make us feel they might have qualified and would have lent themselves admirably to such a process of history-making; for instance, the moment in Egypt when Yahweh separated his people from the others and sent them into the desert to develop into his own people; or again, when Yahweh called Abraham, parted him from friends and relations, and sent him all alone along the way Yahweh had mapped out for him. Israel does not appear to have felt any need to link her election with a definite moment in the past, possibly because she experienced her election above all as a current event in the present. The fact that she had been elected was obviously far more important to her than the election itself — and rightly so.

This awareness of ancient Israel is not, however, uniformly expressed. The fact that already the Patriarchs — especially Jacob, i.e., Israel — had been chosen by Yahweh seems to have been emphasized right from the start. We read, for instance, in Ps. 135:3-5: "Praise the Lord, for the Lord is good; sing to his name, for he is gracious! For the Lord has chosen Jacob for himself, Israel for his own possession. For I know that the Lord is great, and that our Lord is above all gods." And in Isa. 41:8-10: "But you, Israel, my servant, Jacob, whom I have chosen, the offspring of Abraham, my friend; you whom I took from the ends of the earth, and called from its farthest corners, saying to you, 'You are my servant, I have chosen you and not cast you off'; fear not, for I am with you, be not dismayed, for I am your God; I will strengthen you, I will help you, I will uphold you with my victorious right hand." But we must not run away with the idea that this refers primarily or even exclusively to Jacob; it refers in the first place to the Israelites represented in their founder Israel; nor should we lose sight of this just because there has been a narrowing-down to Jacob. It is no different really in the case of a second narrowing-down — of much later date probably — this time to David:

He rejected the tent of Joseph, he did not choose the tribe of Ephraim; but he chose the tribe of Judah, Mount Zion, which he loves. He built his sanctuary like the high heavens, like the earth, which he has founded for ever. He chose David

his servant, and took him from his sheepfolds; from tending
the ewes that had young he brought him to be the shepherd
of Jacob his people, of Israel his inheritance. [Ps. 78:67-71]

This thought recurs in many passages, even in the
historical books (for instance, 1 Kings 8:16). But the
matter here is not entirely the same as it was with
Jacob; as the founder of Israel he really was the
representative of the people; Judah, on the other
hand, was chosen from the people and David from
the tribe of Judah, though his election was for the
benefit of the people. In his case, therefore, we
have a true narrowing-down; which can be graphi-
cally represented as a triangle with the whole of
Israel forming the base, the tribe of Judah the hypot-
eneuse and David himself the apex. This makes it
plain that even among the chosen ones there is a
definite order, and it is just as plain that David's
election must also mean the election of his dynasty
(see, for instance, Ps. 132). Thus David's generation itself becomes the base of a new triangle whose
apex is ultimately formed by the one whom a voice
from heaven called "my chosen Son." (Luke 9:35)

What is the tangible effect on Israel of being chos-
en by God? There is, at any rate, the mutual bond
which, on either side, has — or at least ought to have
— something exclusive about it. We find the plainest
expression of this in Deuteronomy which — more
than any other book — has Israel's election as its
focal point. Chapter 4:32-40 clearly brings out both
the foundation of Israel's election and the reciprocal
bond resulting from it. We read, among other things:

"For ask now of the days that are past, which were before you, since the day that God created man upon the earth, and ask from one end of heaven to the other, whether such a great thing as this has ever happened or was ever heard of. Did any people ever hear the voice of a god speaking out of the midst of the fire, as you have heard, and still live? Or has any god ever attempted to go and take a nation for himself from the midst of another nation, by trials, by signs, by wonders, and by war, by a mighty hand and an outstretched arm, and by great terrors, according to all that the Lord your God did for you in Egypt before your eyes? To you it was shown, that you might know that the Lord is God; there is no other besides him . . . And because he loved your fathers and chose their descendants after them, and brought you out of Egypt with his own presence, by his great power, driving out before you nations greater and mightier than yourselves, to bring you in, to give you their land for an inheritance, as at this day; know therefore this day, and lay it to your heart, that the Lord is God in heaven above and on the earth beneath; there is no other. Therefore you shall keep his statutes and his commandments, which I command you this day, that it may go well with you, and with your children after you, and that you may prolong your days in the land which the Lord your God gives you for ever.

Of all peoples, Israel was the one to be chosen. She was placed in a favorite position because Yahweh regarded her as his child. All that can be said in explanation is that Yahweh loves her. But why? God's love is inexplicable and supreme, like God himself; this is what we are sharply brought up against: the mystery, the complete enigma, before which man can do no other than bow his head.

Did the other peoples then fall outside the orbit of Yahweh's love? Certainly, in the intimate relationship between Yahweh and his people there was no place for them as peoples; but does that also mean that they had to do without Yahweh's love? It would undoubtedly appear so now and again, especially where we read of Egypt's punishment for refusing to let Israel depart; or of Yahweh's command to his chosen ones to wipe out the population of Canaan. And yet is was not so, though it was to take centuries to become clear. At first, indeed, Israel must still take up fixed positions in the Promised Land — but this was only a transition period. She must make a fixed place in her heart for Yahweh, the God she must love. In this connection the existence of the Canaanite population presented a great danger. Only when Israel had made her election reality, could the purpose of it all become plain; first, she must, by her own effort, carry out Yahweh's plans; she must grow into a holy people, a secluded community belonging exclusively to Yahweh. Hence this demand for — provisionally — absolute closedness. Only afterwards could the time arrive for her to open up towards the world.

It is immediately obvious that the awareness of her election brought along great dangers for Israel, to which she often succumbed. Not only was she inclined to forget that being elected made demands on her, but quite often the consciousness that she had been elected by God made her haughty towards the others, and easily gave her the idea that it raised her above the other peoples. Hence Deuteronomy's pointed remark:

For you are a people holy to the Lord your God; the Lord

your God has chosen you to be a people for his own possession, out of all the peoples that are on the face of the
earth. It was not because you were more in number than any
other people that the Lord set his love upon you and chose
you, for you were the fewest of all peoples; but it is because
the Lord loves you, and is keeping the oath which he swore
to your fathers, that the Lord has brought you out with a
mighty hand, from the house of bondage, from the hand of
Pharaoh king of Egypt. See p. 77 — [7:6-2]

This is followed by a renewed call for faithfulness
to Yahweh and his commandments; which proves that
Israel need give herself no airs. There was not the
slightest occasion for it, since it was no thanks to her
if she was Yahweh's elect but thanks only to Yahweh's love and faithfulness. The thought that because
of her election Yahweh would show her more toler-
ance, was also radically rejected. It was not for
nothing that Deuteronomy repeatedly threatened
heavy punishment; and the prophet Amos even expressly underlined that Israel's sins would be punished all the more severely because she was God's
chosen one: "You only have I known of all the families on the earth; therefore I will punish you for all
your iniquities." (Amos. 3:2)

It was especially the Prophets who waged a cease-
less battle against a false conception of the election.
They had to fight slogans like: "Is not the Lord in
the midst of us? No evil shall come upon us" (Mic.
3:11), which they countered with the argument that
Israel would be afflicted with great disasters because
of her unfaithfulness to Yahweh. Well did they realize that her very separation from the masses and

her union with the holy God, Yahweh, made it im-
perative that Israel should be a people of saints,
worthy of her place with Yahweh; and this is why
they never neglected an opportunity to call for a way
of life that would be pleasing to God and for obedience in religious matters. Deuteronomy, for instance, does so in several places: the election, it says,
was not only a gift but also a task, and whoever
remains satisfied with the gift alone, thinks he pos-
sesses something when he really has nothing; for in
the end the gift is there for the sake of the task it
imposes. This again was not obvious at first sight
but needed centuries of reflection and listening to
God's word. Initially it seemed that the task was no
more than remaining faithful to Yahweh and his
commandments; at first, indeed, Israel would not
even have been able to carry out any other task, for
she needed many centuries in which to struggle for
the ability to carry out this one with any semblance
of efficiency. So long as this faithfulness was lacking,
Israel was unable to perform her real mission and
ultimately it was to be no more than a small remnant
of the faithful who were fully prepared for it. We
stand here on the borderline of the election: wher-
ever faithfulness did not materialize, the election was
forfeited, if not by the entire people, at least by the
unfaithful and the lapsed. During the same period
Israel's mission with the other peoples was to be only
a negative one:

When the Lord your God gives them over to you, and you
defeat them; then you must utterly destroy them; you shall
make no covenant with them, and show no mercy to them.

You shall not make marriages with them, giving your daughters to their sons or taking their daughters for your sons. For they would turn away your sons from following me, to serve other gods; then the anger of the Lord would be kindled against you, and he would destroy you quickly. But thus shall you deal with them: you shall break down their altars, and dash in pieces their pillars, and hew down their Asherim, and burn their graven images with fire. [Deut. 7:2-5]

These words are a judgment on the pagans: God has left them to their idolatry and raised only Israel to be the people to serve him:

Beware lest you lift up your eyes to heaven, and when you see the sun and the moon and the stars, all the host of heaven, you be drawn away and worship them and serve them, things which the Lord your God has allotted to all the peoples under the whole heaven. But the Lord has taken you, and brought you forth out of the iron furnace, out of Egypt, to be a people of his own possession, as at this day. [Deut. 4:19-20]

Therefore Israel must conquer them.

But this negative attitude towards the pagans was only a passing one; ultimately it was to become positive and Israel's religious reserve was to open out towards the pagans. The author of the second half of the book of Isaiah brings this out very lucidly:

Behold my servant, whom I uphold, my chosen, in whom my soul delights; I have put my Spirit upon him, he will bring forth justice to the nations. He will not cry or lift up his voice, or make it heard in the street; a bruised reed he will not break, and a dimly burning wick he will not quench; he will faithfully bring forth justice. He will not fail or be discouraged till he has established justice in the earth; and

the coastlands wait for his law. Thus says God, the Lord,
who created the heavens . . . "I am the Lord, I have called
you in righteousness, I have taken you by the hand and kept
you; I have given you as a covenant to the people, a light to
the nations [i.e. the pagans]." [Isa. 42:1-6]

This brought Israel's awareness of being chosen by
Yahweh to a fullness and ripeness beyond further
improvement, which only awaited realization. It was
clear from the outset that the source of Israel's election was Yahweh's love and, whereas at that time it
seemed to be aimed exclusively at Israel, now its aim
was shown to be universal, so that through the Chos-
en People, all were to have access to Yahweh's love.
Now it was more than ever clear that Israel had been
chosen, not because of herself but because through
her, Yahweh wanted to carry out his plans for all
peoples. Therefore the stage in which the election
was an exclusive privilege of Israel, was only a passing one, directed towards a second phase in which
it was to become clear that in principle nobody was
barred. But the question why it was precisely Israel
which was made his instrument, why Israel was the
first to receive Yahweh's grace, brings us once again
before the mystery of Yahweh, who says: "I will be
gracious to whom I will be gracious, and will show
mercy on whom I will show mercy." (Exod. 33:19)

9

THE PROMISE

From time to time the reader will come across the word "promise" in his translation of the Old Testament — without even looking for it — but if he could pick up the Hebrew original he would search in vain for the term. It does not appear in it, because, unlike modern languages, Hebrew has no separate word for it. Does this mean that the concept was just as unknown; or that it was not used where God was concerned? If so, we should be strongly tempted to consider it a specifically Christian term. But even in the books of the New Testament, God's promise is mentioned sparingly and almost exclusively in St. Paul and his disciple Luke. It seems therefore to be peculiar to Paul, though even he never speaks of the Promise in the specifically Christian sense found in later Christian authors where they contrast the Old and New Testaments as the times of promise and fulfillment, expressly noting that the New Testament brings the fulfillment of God's promises in the Old. This simplified presentation is easy enough to understand if Jesus is regarded as the fulfillment of all Yawweh's promises to his elect. It remains a simplification for all that, for even the Old Testament witnessed the fulfillment of an important part of Yah-

weh's promises; nor did Jesus' appearance among us
bring everything to its accomplishment, so that the
Christian too can be said — to a certain extent — to
be living in a time of partial non-fulfillment and to be
hoping still for the full realization of God's promises.
When St. Paul speaks of the promise, he regards it as
a contrast with the law of Moses. Though both came
from God, he regards the promise as the symbol of
God's supreme grace and the law of Moses as that
of man's self-righteousness, since the observance of
the Law easily leads to the presumption that one is
working out one's own holiness; a presumption common in the pious upper crust of Jewry.

It would be unfair to conclude from the absence
of one particular word that Israel was not conscious
of being the bearer of Yahweh's promise. The reverse
is true, though that awareness was only marginal to
the awareness of God. The dynamism of Israel's view
of history and the keen expectation of the future
which is characteristic of the religious Jew's attitude
to life, derive from the very knowledge that he has
received from Yahweh a divine word which is his
guarantee for the future. The fact that this divine
word remains — wholly or partly — unfulfilled, naturally entails a keen expectation of its fulfillment. This
is why the Israelite never settled down completely
in the present but kept an eye on the future, from
which so much was expected. It is not surprising,
then, that the word of the prophet often contains a
promise. Indeed, the prophet may well be a preacher,
but not only does he call his listeners or readers to
a life that is pleasing to God; he nearly always lends

force to his preaching by holding out the prospect of punishment and disaster, but also of deliverance and salvation. And he does it in such a way that his last word is always one of salvation, so that in the end the future is always favorable to those who are converted to Yahweh. Thus there often shines forth from the word of the prophet an optimism — a very remarkable kind at that — which is based on the guarantee of the divine word.

It may be true then to say that the promise forms an integral part of the prophet's preaching. Indeed, the fact that the prophecies contain so many divine words about the future has led many to the misunderstanding that the prophet's first task is foretelling the future. Though this is not correct, the frequency with which they point to the future shows, nevertheless, to what a large extent the religious life of ancient Israel was guided by hope and expectation. To get an idea of this frequency one has only to open Scripture at the collection of prophecies grouped under the name of Isaiah. The call to repentance is often linked with a threat but invariably associated with the prospect of final salvation.

Thus the Old Testament — regarded as one great prophecy — is full of promises but special importance has been attached to two promises which, in a sense, coincide with two turning-points in Israel's history. These, more than any others, have lived on and defined that history. The first of these important events is the election of Abraham and his answer to Yahweh's call, and whoever was responsible for recording it obviously regarded it as a turning-point

in history. Humanity having frequently rejected the
grace he intended for her, Yahweh now made a new
plan: he set apart Abraham to form a new people
out of him, one that would faithfully serve him and
be instrumental in carrying out his plans. All this
we find extensively described in the series of stories
in Gen. 12ff whose author took so deep an interest
in Abraham because of his religious significance.
Yahweh's plan is summarized in his promises to
Abraham; the calling and election itself is formulated as a promise:

Go from your country and your kindred and your father's
house to the land that I will show you. And I will make
of you a great nation, and I will bless you, and make your
name great, so that you will be a blessing. I will bless those
who bless you, and him who curses you I will curse; and by
you all the families of the earth shall bless themselves.
[Gen. 12:1-3]

These are the actual elements of the promise: God
will make Abraham's race into a great people and
through this people — thus we can certainly interpret it — Yahweh's blessing on Abraham will also
fall to the share of all humanity.

In several passages a new element is added, for
instance in 13:15-17:

All the land which you see I will give to you and to your
descendants for ever. I will make your descendants as the dust
of the earth; so that if one can count the dust of the earth,
your descendants also can be counted. Arise, walk through
the length and the breadth of the land, for I will give it to you.

What is so remarkable is that here one of the other

elements drops out; no longer is there any mention of a blessing on all. It is striking, moreover, that we now meet this in every formulation of the promise (15:5; 15:18-19 and even in the extensive rendering of Chapter 17 which represents this reality in terms of the Covenant) except, perhaps, in the formulation of the promise which we find at the crux of the stories, viz., when Abraham has given proof of his faithfulness to Yahweh and Yahweh says to him:

By myself I have sworn, says the Lord, because you have done this, and have not withheld your son, your only son, I will indeed bless you, and I will multiply your descendants as the stars of heaven and as the sand which is on the seashore. And your descendants shall possess the gate of their enemies [that is, shall receive in possession the land that is now in the hands of their enemies], and by your descendants shall all the nations of the earth bless themselves, because you have obeyed my voice. [Gen. 22:16-18]

These promises are also incorporated in the cycle of the stories concerning Jacob. (Gen. 28:13-15; 35:11-13)

It is not surprising that later on special attention was paid to those elements of the promise whose fulfillment lay — in a certain measure — in the people's own hands, particularly the conquest of the Promised Land, which they considered themselves entitled to on the strength of Yahweh's word. This is the clue to the motivation of Israel's history — or at least of the recording of that history. Up to the time of Moses, Abraham's sons needed all their powers to grow into a sizeable group of men who were then united into a real people by a great spiritual leader and derived

from the hardships commonly endured in the desert
the solidarity necessary for growing into a real community. There followed then a period which was to
see the fulfillment of the second part of the promise:
the occupation of Canaan, the land to which Yahweh's promise entitled them and where the purchase
of a plot of ground at Machpelah had already given
Abraham initial property rights. The basic element
was the awareness of people and leaders that this
land was the territory set aside by Yahweh for ancient
Israel, an awareness expressed in the stories of the
promise which, in their turn, gave this consciousness
its impulse and retained its stimulus in the course
of history, as witness the frequent references to this
promise.

When the land had been conquered and its possession consolidated, the promise lost some of its
stimulating and driving effect; not because it had
now been completely fulfilled but because it was
anything but clear how its unfulfilled portion (God's
blessing on the whole earth through Abraham's seed)
was to be achieved. Obviously this tended to weaken
the people's enthusiasm. Just then a new promise
was mentioned. When David had thoroughly beaten
the Philistines and finally managed to mould the
twelve tribes into an administrative unit governed
from a common capital, Jerusalem, a divine word
was addressed to him, which was also to give rise to
considerable expectation. In 2 Sam. 7 this divine
word is related to David's plan to build a great temple for Yahweh and forms part of a much longer
prophecy of Nathan:

The Lord declares to you that the Lord will make you a
house. When your days are fulfilled and you lie down with
your fathers, I will raise up your offspring after you, who
shall come forth from your body, and I will establish his
kingdom. He shall build a house for my name, and I will
establish the throne of his kingdom for ever. I will be his
father, and he shall be my son. When he commits⸃ iniquity,
I will chasten him with the rod of men, with the stripes of
the sons of men; but I will not take my steadfast love from
him, as I took it from Saul, whom I put away from before
you. And your house and your kingdom shall be made sure
for ever before me; your throne shall be established for ever.
[*vv.* 12-16; see also 1 Chron. 17:10-14 which has the same
context, and Ps. 2 which, in my opinion, is inspired by the
same promise.]

This promise has, therefore, no direct bearing on
the whole people, but only on the tribe of David (as
king, yet another representative of Israel); at any rate,
it is narrowed down here. Moreover, it gives far less
concrete detail; all it says is that David's generation
will reign forever. But how was that to come about?
Particularly after Jerusalem had been taken, in 586,
this must have been a great problem. The answer is
the expectation of the son of David, the issue of
David or of a new David. We need labor this no
further; we can content ourselves by merely noting
that the promise to David offered firm support to
the expectation that a personal saviour would restore
what was so painfully lacking formerly and lead
Israel's history to new and permanent heights.

Thus we see Yahweh's promises crystallizing around
two points, two important events, in history. Remark-
ably enough the first lies outside, i.e., before, Israel's

history proper. After all, she only began her existence as a real people in Moses' time, and accordingly this promise is, before anything else, a promise to the community which has not yet been moulded into a people. In brief, bold outlines, Israel's greatest ancestor (and therefore Israel herself, the seed of Abraham) is given a glimpse of her history and role; and once again there is now a person who officially represents the people, though in a somewhat different way. For this reason the promise to the king can also be a promise to the whole people; but, for all that, this narrowing-down to the generation of David undoubtedly holds the seed of the hopeful expectation of a personal saviour and judge.

10

THE COVENANT

Not just on the periphery but at the very center of the awareness of God in the Old Testament we find a concept which has its roots in a particular event and can, therefore, only be properly understood if viewed from a certain moment in Israel's history: the Covenant. If we are to examine the place of the Covenant in Israel's awareness of God it will not be sufficient for us just to analyze the meaning of the term. Although this is plain enough when translated, it is altogether different to the term found in the Hebrew original, since it is difficult to determine its original root.

There is no doubt, however, about the place the Covenant occupied in ancient Israel's daily life — as well as in that of all the peoples who led or had led a nomadic existence in the Near East. For these nomadic tribes, life and safety were only assured within the narrow family circle and the tribal association with which they had blood ties. However, the traditions and customs guaranteeing justice and legal security only affected members of the tribe; those who fell outside this narrow circle were, of necessity, enemies and as such, without rights. Adoption into this judicial community was conditional upon entry

into the community of life which was its foundation.
Now, an outsider could only join by making a covenant which gave him a measure of recognition as a
blood relation and fellow tribesman and granted
membership of the great community. Apart from a
solemn declaration — often sealed with an oath —
this recognition was confirmed by various rites, such
as joining in a communal meal, and different kinds
of blood ceremonies in which, for instance, the blood
of the tribal chief and that of the covenanter were
allowed to mingle.

Naturally the Israel we know had already out-
grown this stage, though various expressions still
seem to remind us of it.

To be properly appreciated the Covenant between
Yahweh and his people must probably be seen against
this background; and the religious awareness that a
covenant had been made between Yahweh and Israel,
therefore, really the consciousness that God and his
people now belonged to the same sphere of life. Like
any other covenant it came about by a kind of bila-
teral agreement, but an agreement of an altogether
different order, in this case, because those who made
it were not equal partners — though it does not alter
the fact that it was freely entered into on both sides.
However, on Yahweh's side the making of the Covenant was sign and proof of his choice; on Israel's
side it was primarily a token of obedient docility. The
immediate effect of the Covenant was the establishment of a state of "peace," not only in the negative
sense that enmity had ceased, but also in the full
sense of the Hebrew word that things were now as

they should be. In Israel's religious usage the Covenant was undoubtedly given a place of major importance and this was of almost universal application. In the eyes of the Israelite it was the central thought, the very one in which the relation between Yahweh and his people was given its purest expression. It is not surprising, therefore, that we find it elaborately developed right through the Scriptures.

Although the ancient Israelite undoubtedly always experienced his union with Yahweh as a living reality, at all times he paid great attention to the moment when the Covenant came into being: the great event on Mount Sinai. Even in Exodus we find several divergent renderings of it (19:24 and ch. 34) and we can detect echoes of it in many other passages. In Chapter 19 Yahweh appears on Mount Sinai amid all sorts of phenomena which clearly bring out the "awfulness" of his mysterious majesty, which make the people shiver and tremble so much that they suggest Moses should approach Yahweh on their behalf. They receive the following reply: "Do not fear; for God has come to prove you, and that the fear of him may be before your eyes, that you may not sin." (Exod. 20:20) The events related in ch. 24 are altogether different; they are less terrifying, less supernatural, more adapted to human categories and human (in this instance Israelite) customs:

Moses came and told the people all the words of the Lord and all the ordinances; and all the people answered with one voice, and said, "All the words which the Lord has spoken we will do." And Moses wrote all the words of the Lord. And he rose early in the morning, and built an altar at the foot of

the mountain, and twelve pillars, according to the twelve
tribes of Israel. And he sent young men of the people of
Israel, who offered burnt offerings and sacrificed peace offerings of oxen to the Lord. And Moses took half of the blood
and put it in basins, and half the blood he threw against the
altar. Then he took the book of the covenant, and read it in
the hearing of the people: and they said, "All that the Lord
has spoken we will do, and we will be obedient." And Moses
took the blood and threw it upon the people, and said,
"Behold the blood of the covenant which the Lord has made
with you in accordance with all these words." Then Moses
and Aaron, Nadab, and Abihu, and seventy of the elders of
Israel went up, and they saw the God of Israel; and there
was under his feet as it were a pavement of sapphire stone,
like the very heaven for clearness. And he did not lay his
hand on the chief men of the people of Israel; they beheld
God, and ate and drank. [Exod. 24:3-11]

The ceremonies described are strongly reminiscent
of contractual practice between men. First the terms
of the contract are solemnly agreed. To this end
Moses reads from the "book of the covenant," the
great charter of the Covenant, the law Israel must
abide by under the terms of this treaty, and the
people express their agreement in an official statement. Then a sacrifice is offered to Yahweh and with
this blood that now belongs to him, the people are
sprinkled, so that Yahweh enters into a communion
of life with the people who, for their part, now be-
long to the same tribal association. Then follows a
meal — no doubt of a sacrificial nature. Chapter 19
shows that Yahweh has made a choice, a selection:

You have seen what I did to the Egyptians, and how I bore
you on eagles' wings and brought you to myself. Now there-

fore, if you will obey my voice and keep my covenant, you shall be my own possession among all peoples; for all the earth is mine, and you shall be to me a kingdom of priests and a holy nation. [*vv.* 4-6]

But for the people too the making of the Covenant is a choice (19:20, cited above), an exclusive one at that, as borne out by the first commandment that Israel must have no strange gods beside Yahweh, and by the order that they are to wipe out the peoples they shall come in contact with in Canaan, because otherwise they will draw Israel away from Yahweh; an ordinance whereby Yahweh has definitely linked the execution of his plans with Israel.

This Covenant was officially and solemnly renewed and ratified on more than one occasion; for instance, by Joshua on Mount Ebal and on Mount Gerizim, where, after their arrival in Canaan, he made the people renew their choice (Joshua 8:30-35; ch. 24); by King Josiah after the finding of the Book of the Covenant (2 Kings 23) and later by Esdras and Nehemias (Neh. 8). This appears to have been called for by repeated cases of unfaithfulness to the Covenant. What is remarkable about it, however, is that Yahweh, who has really made his selection dependent on the condition that Israel remains faithful to him, never denounces the treaty and remains faithful even in the darkest moments of Israel's history, though it often seems to be the reverse. Indeed, when he sends his punishments he only does so to bring the people to repentance and to renew their ties.

Israel's theology regards the Covenant as the heart of the religious life and so strongly does it hold this

view that various events before the making of the
Covenant on Sinai are also described as covenants.
For instance, the promise to Abraham is also called
a covenant (Gen. 17), the circumcision being its sign
and seal (Gen. 17:11) and similarly the promise to
Noah is described as a covenant which Yahweh
makes with him, the sign in this case being the rain-
bow. (Gen. 9)

It is Jeremiah who finally opens up the prospect
of a time when the Covenant is to be renewed in
such a way that there can no longer be any question
of unfaithfulness; when the Covenant is to be a permanent union, never to be broken by the people
either, because this time will see the Law engraved
on their hearts and any conflict between the desires
of the heart and the demands of the law brought to
an end:

Behold, the days are coming, says the Lord, when I will
make a new covenant with the house of Israel and the house
of Judah, not like the covenant which I made with their
fathers when I took them by the hand to bring them out of
the land of Egypt, my covenant which they broke, though I
was their husband, says the Lord. But this is the covenant
which I will make with the house of Israel after those days,
says the Lord: I will put my law within them, and I will
write it upon their hearts; and I will be their God, and they
shall be my people. And no longer shall each man teach his
neighbor and each his brother, saying, "Know the Lord," for
they shall all know me, from the least of them to the greatest,
says the Lord; for I will forgive their iniquity, and I will
remember their sin no more. [Jer. 31:31-34]

11

YAHWEH, THE KING

It would be astonishing if Israel's awareness of God had not been sensibly affected by her golden age — as we usually call the first century of the monarchy, the rise under Saul, the climax under David and the beginning of Solomon's reign. Texts of later date prove that Israel has fed on it for centuries, not only when, independent at least in theory, she was experiencing the decline of the kingdom, but also during and after her exile when there was no longer any question of independence.

There is reason to assume that Israel had already been honoring Yahweh as her King before; indeed, she was not alone in doing so, since it appears to have been the universal practice of the Semitic races; some people even went so far as to call their god "king" as though it were a surname. The Semitic word *melech* ("king") is easily recognizable in the Accadian god Malik and the Phoenician Melkart. Even in Israel the name was not unknown; we think of the name Molech — corrupted to Moloch, a god (maybe a Phoenician one) to whom children were sacrificed. (2 Kings 23:10; Jer. 32:35; see also Lev. 17 and 20) In ancient Israel also there were people who bore surnames in which God was indicated as melech, king. But, we may ask, had they not simply borrowed those names from their environment without adopting their meaning?

Originally the name "king" seems to have been applied to Yahweh in the sense of "protector," "guide" or "leader" (in the narrow sense of the term: the one who led Israel out of Egypt) for instance in the ancient song in Exod. 15:1-20: "The Lord will reign for ever and ever. For when the horses of Pharaoh with his chariots and his horsemen went into the sea, the Lord brought back the waters of the sea upon them; but the people of Israel walked on dry ground in the midst of the sea." (*vv.* 18-19) This general sense is, after all, still found in later ages.

The foundation of a kingdom in Israel undoubtedly stimulated the desire to apply this title more emphatically to Yahweh, and this was done by contrasting the political kingship with Yahweh's — often so forcefully that in some circles the desire for a king was regarded as a betrayal of Yahweh: "But the thing displeased Samuel when they said, 'Give us a king to govern us.' And Samuel prayed to the Lord. And the Lord said to Samuel, 'Hearken to the voice of the people in all that they say to you; for they have not rejected you, but they have rejected me from being king over them.'" (1 Sam. 8:6-7)

Yahweh's kingship seems to have been repeatedly celebrated, especially in the temple rites; a practice which may have been connected with the knowledge that Yahweh was present in the temple as the King, sitting on his throne, his feet resting on the Ark as his footstool. This explains why the vision in which

Yahweh showed himself to Isaiah as a king took place in the temple: "I saw the Lord sitting upon a throne, high and lifted up; and his train filled the temple." (Isa. 6:1) When the people of Israel assembled in the temple, they knew they were united around the throne of the King: "Lift up your heads, O gates! and be lifted up, O ancient doors! that the King of glory may come in. Who is the King of glory? The Lord, strong and mighty, the Lord, mighty in battle!" (Ps. 24:7-8) Public worship honored him as the King.

Many of the songs used in these devotions have been bequeathed to us in the Psalms — songs which may well have been collected in a separate book, since most of them are similarly grouped in the present arrangement of the Psalter, as we can easily observe for ourselves (Ps. 93-99 and perhaps also 100)

It is remarkable that, apart from public worship, Yahweh was seldom given the title of King. What could have been the reason behind this? Maybe because royal titles were so copiously lavished on all sorts of other gods who, from Israel's point of view, were only fakes. Maybe also because it was thought undesirable to bring Yahweh under one common denominator with the bearers of the political kingship. For the period in which everyone could plainly detect in the kings the requisite grandeur, cheek by jowl with abject misery, was a relatively short one, certainly from the religious point of view. What even grandees like Saul, David and Solomon had to show was anything but a reflection of Yahweh's kingship. However, when the kingdom had been divided and the religious decline of the monarchy definitely set in, there was every reason for not drawing too close a parallel between Yahweh and these kings who, from the religious angle at any rate, appeared to be failures. But this reserve does not alter the fact that Yahweh's kingship was often hymned in the services of the Temple.

Even among exegetes there are those who hold the opinion that Israel — like Babylon — celebrated some kind of festival of God's enthronement, in connection with the feast of the new year. The special rites of this feast are said to have consisted of a reading of the story of the Creation, a religious drama representing Yahweh's fight with his enemies as an actual occurrence, a solemn procession (probably with the Ark) and a new enthronement of Yahweh, whereby he signified his renewed acceptance of power. There is no specific mention of such a feast anywhere in the Old Testament, but it cannot be denied that it is precisely in the "royal" psalms that we read about processions and a solemn entry of Yahweh (Ps. 24), a conquest over his enemies, Yahweh's creative power, even his enthronement and his assumption of the kingship. (Ps. 47, 93, 97, and 99) There may be no decisive arguments for the existence of such a feast, but it can hardly be denied that it was precisely in the temple services — or in some of them at least — that this kingship regained its real character in the eyes of the Israelites. We shall find this easier to understand if we bear in mind that Yahweh's kingship was considered to be active and not static. Time and again Yahweh manifested his kingship in mighty deeds and demonstrations of benevo-

lence to Israel; and thus every powerful deed on
Yahweh's part came to be regarded as a new confir-
mation and execution of his kingship. Moreover, the
community's renewed witness to these mighty deeds
in its prayers and songs of praise meant a re-
establishment of Yahweh's kingship.

The solution to the question of the inner meaning
of Yahweh's kingship is not so easily found and it is
to be found almost exclusively in the Psalms. Naturally there is a direct link between Yahweh's kingship
and his great power. This was originally experienced
merely as Yahweh's favor towards Israel, and while
it lasted God was seen exclusively as Israel's King,
who led the people in such a way that, with his help,
it was able to triumph over the other peoples. This
is clearly borne out, for instance, in the above-quoted
passage from Exod. 15:18-19 or in the words of the
prophet Zephaniah: "The Lord has taken away the
judgments against you, he has cast out your enemies.
The King of Israel, the Lord, is in your midst; you
shall fear evil no more." (3:15)

It was only in the post-exilic period that the consciousness dawned that Yahweh must reign as King
over all the earth: "And the Lord will become king
over all the earth; on that day the Lord will be one
and his name one." (Zech. 14:9) This is the tenor of
most of the "royal" psalms: "Say among the nations,
'The Lord reigns!' Yea, the world is established, it
shall never be moved; he will judge the peoples with
equity." (Ps. 96:10) Yahweh's mighty deeds will
then be known to all peoples and all the earth will
recognize his kingship — in the words of Ps. 98.

Even the universe joins in this homage, the streams clap their hands and the mountains shout for joy. This is no annulment of Israel's election, for it is precisely because Yahweh lives up to his choice that all will understand what he means to Israel and to all mankind.

Accordingly there is — to my way of thinking — good reason for pointing out a few of the differences in the way Yahweh's kingship was regarded before and after the Exile. Before the Exile, when Yahweh was held to be the King of Israel, the dominating factor was the thought that Yahweh was Israel's saviour and helper who assisted her in her fight against the other peoples. When the Exile had broadened Israel's outlook and Yahweh's kingship was no longer limited to his chosen people, the emphasis fell more on the glitter, the glory and the magnificence of his kingship. It could perhaps be said that, whereas he was formerly thought of predominantly as Israel's army commander, he was now regarded as the director of all mankind, indeed of everything that took place in the world and the whole universe.

Was Yahweh's kingship invariably felt to be an actuality? Certainly in the sense that the foundation of his kingship had already taken place, but probably not in the sense that he was already exercising his power over all the earth and that his kingship was receiving general recognition. In a sense God's kingship was indeed real, but because it was not universally manifested yet, it did not always receive recognition. Time and again both aspects are brought into relief.

12

THE FULFILLMENT

One of the striking features of the Scriptures is that, whereas Yahweh is regularly referred to as the King, his kingship or kingdom are hardly ever mentioned; and yet it is the central thought, not only of the New Testament but also of the apocryphal books that precede it. And what of the Old Testament; is the conception lacking there just as its expression is also lacking? Certainly not, for it is implicit in the mere fact of calling Yahweh King.

In the course of Israel's history there was — as I have already underlined — only a partial realization of God's kingship. Hence the longing for the time — in the far-off future, of course — which was to see the full realization of God's kingship. But for Israel that future did, nevertheless, have a well defined beginning: experience and wisdom gained from the Prophets made her understand that complete fulfillment was not to be achieved through human efforts alone and that it would not fit into the normal run of history. Consequently the day that witnessed it would be "the day of the Lord"; one which, through his intervention, was to bring a decisive turn of events.

In this decisive turn Yahweh's kingship would play

the dominant part, as Isa. 52:7, more perhaps than
any other passage, so clearly expresses: "How beautiful upon the mountains are the feet of him who
brings good tidings, who publishes peace, who brings
good tidings of good, who publishes salvation, who
says to Zion, 'Your God reigns.'" It us understandable then that all the hopes and expectations of that
day are best termed "God's kingdom."

Its establishment would be preceded by God's
judgment on pagans and Israelites who would perish
as a result of God's punishments, with a remnant
coming to repentance, thus inaugurating a period
of happiness and prosperity. This is just one way of
looking at it. There are, in fact, so many complicated
and divergent conceptions that it is impossible to
summarize them briefly. What does clearly emerge
is the certainty for most Israelites that in the end
all would come right. Especially in times of decline
and preoccupation with the external trappings of
religious worship — without a corresponding inward
disposition and a way of life that pleased God — this
attitude drew protests from the Prophets; for instance,
Amos:

> Woe to you who desire the day of the Lord! Why would
> you have the day of the Lord? It is darkness, and not light;
> as if a man fled from a lion, and a bear met him; or went
> into the house and leaned with his hand against the wall, and
> a serpent bit him. Is not the day of the Lord darkness, and
> not light, and gloom with no brightness in it? [v. 18-20]

Yet even Amos sees this darkness as a passage towards the light (ch. ix): in the end Yahweh will

"raise up the booth of David that is fallen" and all will be repaired. Prosperity and happiness will be Israel's share and nothing will ever change this again.

The day of the Lord will bring history to an end. If, until then, Yahweh has used man's actions to achieve his plans, he will on that day interrupt the normal run of history and intervene personally: he will manifest himself with all the richness of his being. Thus the day will be one of many aspects: Yahweh's words and deeds will — more than ever before — bring judgment and punishment, but also salvation and redemption; everything he has so far done will appear to have been only provisional, and will be followed by the final judgment, the final punishment, but also the final salvation and that redemption which will never again be forfeited.

All this has a primarily collective bearing. In almost all the Prophets we find extensive pronouncements affecting peoples as a whole; a strong argument in favor of the great antiquity of these notions and, at the same time, an explanation of the Israelites' light-heartedness in presuming upon their election and considering themselves beyond all possible harm. Later on this was considerably modified, the view being that Israel would be punished just as much — if not more severely — and that only a remnant would be saved. The other peoples too would receive their due punishment but they would also have their share in redemption and salvation. Most prophets, indeed, portray how they will go to Jerusalem and there — in the company of those Israelites who were saved — give praise and honor to Yahweh. It is only then that songs of praise like Ps. 96, 98, and 99 will be fully applicable. And the acts of worship in the Temple are, therefore, not only a celebration of God's wonders come true again, but also an anticipation of his final intervention. On that day the infinitely exalted God will be nearer than ever before; his words and deeds will be mightier than ever and his coming will be as it never was before. His promises will be fulfilled without any reserve and he will really stand by his covenant in full measure and all men will be his confederates and allies. Only then will Yahweh's kingship attain its full inner meaning.

It is notable, however, that whilst the strongest emphasis is everywhere placed on Yahweh's personal intervention when that day comes, and every attention is fixed on him alone, there still remains room for another king. Indeed, the happy period following the day of the Lord, which will bring back all that was admirable in the past and made Israel glorious, will also restore the kingship. And the memory of David seems so green that the new king is invariably connected with him and drawn in traits which are nearly all taken from David's portrait.

Already during his lifetime David was given this promise through the prophet Nathan: "When your days are fulfilled and you lie down with your fathers, I will raise up your offspring after you, who shall come forth from your body, and I will establish his kingdom . . . And your house and your kingdom shall be made sure for ever before me; your throne shall be established for ever." (2 Sam. 7:12-16) Because of the conviction that Yahweh's ways had been mapped out from all eternity, this line of thought was projected back into history so that the prophet Balaam (Num. 24:17) and even Jacob, the founder of the tribe of Israel, were made to foretell this: "The scepter shall not depart from Judah, nor the ruler's staff from between his feet, until he comes to whom it belongs; and to him shall be the obedience of the peoples." (Gen. 49:10) Again and again great play is made with this thought: when Israel has been restored to glory after the day of the Lord — in Yahweh's own words, expressed through Amos: "I will raise up the booth of David that is fallen and repair its breaches, and raise up its ruins, and rebuild it as in the days of old; that they may possess the remnant of Edom and all the nations who are called by my name." (9:1-12)

The prophecy of peace and unity in the kingdom when that time comes and the statement that the new king will be born in Bethlehem and that even as a child he will be King, are things that remind us of David. It even seems likely that the many allusions to the fact that he will appear as a shepherd point to David, the shepherd's boy:

My servant David shall be king over them; and they shall all have one shepherd. They shall follow my ordinances and be careful to observe my statutes. They shall dwell in the land where your fathers dwelt that I gave to my servant Jacob; they and their children and their children's children shall dwell there for ever; and David my servant shall be their prince for ever. I will make a covenant of peace with them; it shall be an everlasting covenant with them; and I will bless them and multiply them, and will set my sanctuary

in the midst of them for evermore. My dwelling place shall
be with them; and I will be their God, and they shall be my
people. Then the nations will know that I the Lord sanctify
Israel, when my sanctuary is in the midst of them for evermore. [Ezek. 37:24-28; see also 34:23ff]

It is clear that a passage like this brings back all
the elements of Israel's awareness of God: Yahweh's
omnipotence, his deeds and words, the election, the
Promise, the Covenant and the Kingdom.

But the perspective in which all this is placed
shows just as plainly the awareness in the best of
Israel's sons that they are living in the Old Testament: God's intervention in Israel's history is never
conclusive; his word is never the last; finality is still
awaited.

In the Christian view this has meanwhile come to
pass: the decisive intervention has been made; the
word on which all converges has been spoken. But
the Christian attitude to life is not entirely focussed
on the present, nor does it try to turn past events
into a thoroughly experienced and effective reality.
The Christian also looks to the future. The decisive
intervention may well have been initiated but it
has not been finalized. The decisive word has been
spoken but not in full. For him too there is still a
Day of the Lord. But he knows that the one who is
to judge and reign with Yahweh has already taken
his place at his right hand in readiness for the day
when he is to return upon the clouds of heaven.